OPEN PROCESS FRAMEWORKS

IEEE Computer Society Publications
The world-renowned IEEE Computer Society publishes, promotes, and distributes a wide variety of authoritative computer science and engineering texts. These books are available from most retail outlets. Visit the CS Store at *http://computer.org/cspress* for a list of products.

IEEE Computer Society / Wiley Partnership
The IEEE Computer Society and Wiley partnership allows the CS Press authored book program to produce a number of exciting new titles in areas of computer science and engineering with a special focus on software engineering. IEEE Computer Society members continue to receive a 15% discount on these titles when purchased through Wiley or at wiley.com/ieeecs

To submit questions about the program or send proposals please e-mail dplummer@computer.org or write to Books, IEEE Computer Society, 100662 Los Vaqueros Circle, Los Alamitos, CA 90720-1314. Telephone +1-714-821-8380.
Additional information regarding the Computer Society authored book program can also be accessed from our web site at *http://computer.org/cspress*

OPEN PROCESS FRAMEWORKS

Patterns for the Adaptive e-Enterprise

With a Case Study in Contract Labor Management

DAVID A. MARCA

University of Phoenix

Foreword by

Walter Bender

MIT Media Lab

A WILEY-INTERSCIENCE PUBLICATION

Library of Congress Cataloging-in-Publication Data is available.

ISBN 10: 0-471-73611-2
ISBN 13: 978-0-471-73611-0

Printed in the United States of America.

10 9 8 7 6 5 4 3 2 1

To Julie

CONTENTS

PART IV: e-PROJECT

FOREWORD

In 1960, J. C. R. Licklider, when considering the relationship between people and computing machines, predicted that, "Men will set the goals, formulate the hypotheses, determine the criteria, and perform the evaluations. Computing machines will do the routinizable work that must be done to prepare the way for insights and decisions in technical and scientific thinking." For the next 20 years, Licklider's prediction seemed to hold true.

The first challenge to Licklider's prediction came in 1979, when Dan Bricklin and Bob Frankston invented VisiCalc, the first computer spreadsheet program, which ran on an Apple II computer. In retrospect, the impact of the spreadsheet is obvious, but at the time it was not as readily adopted by the business community as one would have thought. Managers looked upon it with disdain, often remarking, "Why should I use this? Isn't this why we have an accounting department?" It took some time before they realized that the spreadsheet was not about balancing the books; it was a projection tool, a "thing to think with," of greater relevance to the strategic processes of the front office than the tactical processes of the back office. Bricklin and Frankston's invention let individual managers partner with the machine to reach levels of complexity unimagined two decades earlier.

The Internet had its beginning in the Arpanet project in the late 1960s. However, it was only with the emergence of the World Wide Web, and the rapid spread of human-to-computer and computer-to-computer communications of the 1990s that it fostered, that a further challenge to Licklider's vision materialized. We have seen the transformation of business communications from a discrete to continuous process. We have also seen the transformation of the value of information interchange into actionable knowledge; not just the capacity and roles of individuals are being transformed, but the entirety of the business ecosystem.

It is exactly this spirit of transformation that is at the core of David Marca's *Open Process Frameworks*. He describes those aspects of the new "process" medium that are the key differentiators for developing successful business strategies. He has developed an approach to building business and supply chain competitiveness through a combination of astute observations of best practices, as well as a comprehensive and comprehensible framework in which to apply them. Marca presents a succinct, pragmatic, step-by-step guide to open process frameworks that includes both what to do and why to do it, followed by real-world examples through which the impact of each step is made evident.

Marca's *Open Process Frameworks*—a vision of the Internet as not just a communication medium, but also as a process medium—takes the symbiosis between organizations and machines to a level unimagined by Licklider, a true partnership that brings adaptability and efficiency to business, with the possibility of nurturing a new era of productivity and growth.

WALTER BENDER
Executive Director
MIT Media Lab

October 8, 2004

PREFACE

Business success in the 21st century will require companies to become highly adaptable. They will need to quickly identify and respond to new business opportunities. They will need to successfully acquire, or merge with, other firms. They will need to rapidly create and change strategic alliances. And they will need to instantly and selectively open and close their core operations to customers, channels, and employees. This kind of business adaptability demands a seamless, flexible, and highly integrated business–process–technology solution using the latest Internet technologies. "Adaptive e-Enterprise" is the name for this kind of solution.

THE ADAPTIVE e-ENTERPRISE

Business executives and managers are working as hard as they can to remain profitable and to see their companies succeed over the long run. This is evidenced by their actions to outsource in order to reduce their cost of operation, and by their actions to create mergers, acquisitions, and strategic alliances to foster growth. But these business initiatives are not always successful, and most do not create the kind of results that were originally expected. A primary reason for these poor results is that companies do not yet have an overall design that enables the easy and rapid creation of business partnerships. In other words, companies are not designed to be highly adaptable—they are not open.

If a business is designed to be entirely open so that each and every aspect of it could potentially be linked to another company, that design would enable the rapid and successful shedding of nonessential activities to other firms so that the business could retain its core competency while spending a minimum for all required support functions. The Internet and its underlying technologies are right now evolving into a set of tools that a business can use to transform itself into an e-enterprise, capable of making adaptable business connections in an extremely short period of time. But this goal cannot be realized unless the business, its process, and its technology are all designed to be open. When the business, process, and technology are open, an adaptive e-enterprise is possible. For example:

- **Open Business.** A business first inherits its industry's accepted standards for terminology and business rules that are defined with XML. After strategic and tactical planning, the firm then adds its own set of enterprise-wide rules (i.e. its policies and operational rules, again written in XML) to the industry standard. The company then defines a compliance and/or performance measure for each XML rule using an Internet-based language such as Java. Since all rules and metrics are coded in a standard way, they can be easily shared, exchanged, or replaced with any other company that has also encoded its business layer in this way.

- **Open Process.** A business defines its operations in terms of the business events it services. It then defines a unique response to each business event. A response is defined as a set of process steps, each one being a distinct Web page capable of being executed by either a person or a machine. Each Web page uses the business's XML rules, and may add its own rules to the corporate standard. Since each process step is a Web page, it can potentially be viewed, accessed, executed, and monitored by any corporate entity. Therefore, corporate executives have the ability to decide, at a moment's notice, which portions of their business to outsource and which to keep proprietary.

- **Open Technology.** Each process Web page may invoke one or more software functions to accomplish its portion of a response to an event. Thus, each software function has two interfaces: one for people and one for machines. The software functions are also autonomous—they are not part of any large (and often proprietary) software application. Since all software functions have Internet-based interfaces, they can be accessed by any process Web page, person, or software function via an Internet, extranet, or intranet connection. This design strategy is also applied to the company's data—they become autonomous objects, each with its own interface that enables direct invocation by any and all process Web pages and software functions.

An Adaptive e-enterprise is a combination of open business, open process, and open technology. This book is a collection of anecdotes, designed to let you simultaneously design business–process–technology openness. It almost seems counterintuitive to design your company to be open. We may resist the notion that success means allowing other firms to know our business. Success in the 20th century was based on confidential business models, hidden operations, and proprietary technology. Success in the 21st century will rely on industry standard business models, open operations, and commoditized technology. Let us keep in mind that an adaptive e-enterprise does not share its core competency. It defines itself so that every aspect that is not core can be outsourced to, merged with, or insourced from other firms. And because it is designed for this purpose, business executives can make adaptability decisions, something they have never been able to do before.

e-BUSINESS, e-PROCESS, e-COMMERCE, AND e-PROJECT

An adaptive e-enterprise is complex. It has many parts. The parts are specialized, and there are many ways to combine them into a final solution. This complexity can be managed, however through the use of patterns. A pattern is a design principle (i.e., a "rule of thumb" or "best practice") that creates one part of a solution. When used in conjunction with other patterns, each part fits perfectly with all the other parts. I wrote this book to share with you those patterns I found most useful in designing seamless, flexible, and highly integrated business–process–technology solutions.

This book is divided into four parts. Part I, e-Business, contains patterns to help with business planning and strategy development. It provides design guidance for organizations and supply chains so they can take full advantage of Internet technology. Part II, e-Process, contains patterns that help with the analysis of business operations and process reengineering. It gives design guidance on translating business process into active Web pages and then linking those Web pages to e-Commerce systems. Part III, e-Commerce, covers software design, but with special emphasis on the Internet technologies and architecture required to achieve adaptability. Part IV, e-Project, addresses project management concerns when implementing highly complex solutions. It thus provides project management anecdotes for conducting an adaptive e-enterprise initiative.

A business–process–technology solution also places new demands on a company's organization. For example, it requires senior management, process architects, software designers, and project managers to work more closely together. It helps them operate like a championship sports team—everyone instinctively knows their position on the field, and everyone knows precisely how each of their teammates will react when a particular situation arises. This book was designed to describe not only an adaptive e-enterprise solution, but the role each party plays in creating that solution:

- Part I, e-Business, is for senior management.
- Part II, e-Process, is for process architects.
- Part III, e-Commerce, is for software designers.
- Part IV, e-Project, is for project managers.

THE INTERNET AS PROCESS MEDIUM

Business adaptability in the 21st century does not require a business to be predominantly "brick-and-mortar" or predominantly Internet-based. Adaptability is the speed at which a company can change itself to stay competitive. This requires sound business–process–technology practices that lead to lasting success (i.e., business durability). Internet technology does enable competitiveness, and, if used to also enable adaptability, it can create long-term business durability. However, using the Internet as a medium to achieve business adaptability is only now starting to gain momentum. The reason for this trend is that, up until now, assumptions about what the Internet is has been shaped by our past notions of media.

This phenomenon of understanding a new medium based on old ones is not new. For example, go back into the television archives, to the very first TV programs. Those very first shows had people physically gathered around microphones reading scripts. They conducted a TV broadcast as if they were on radio! The only thing different was that the viewers saw the radio program participants, instead of just hearing them. The use of TV changed only when people understood the power of TV as a visual medium for advertising. This phenomenon was repeated for the Internet: Companies have so far used the Internet based on their understanding of prior media: television, telephones, and encyclopedias. This means that the time interval between the emergence of the Internet and its full utilization will be roughly the same as for other media (i.e., decades).

Evidence abounds for the theory that current uses of the Internet come from our under-standing of the aforementioned traditional media (e.g., pop-up ads, chat rooms, targeted e-mail, search strings, and so on). And it is this fundamental thinking that created the first understanding of what electronic commerce is—a medium for advertising or brokering that leads to purchases. To state this metaphor in a different way, "Let's use the Internet like we do television or printed media—to advertise—and let consumers purchase online after they read the ad." This metaphor has utility, but it lacks a perspective that enables adaptability—process.

THE OPEN PROCESS CONCEPT

This book suggests an additional metaphor for the Internet—that the Internet is a medium quite different from its predecessors. The Internet can be thought of as a process medium, as opposed to an advertising medium, a transactional medium, or an informational medi-um. To view the Internet in this way is to make a shift in how to utilize it to conduct busi-ness, how to develop software to support a business so its potential for adaptability is maximized, and how to actually be highly responsive to the evolving needs of a business. Therefore, this book is about taking a glimpse into the Internet's hidden value—one that enables a business to gain operational efficiencies without being overconstrained by regu-latory standards, to better link to customers and suppliers, and to quickly adapt to chang-ing market conditions without being constrained by software.

The key to adaptive e-enterprise design is linking business plans and strategies directly to e-commerce systems via a business process that has been fully implemented with Inter-net technology. This value is realized when the operational processes of a business are carefully designed and implemented as a set of interdependent Web pages that match the structure of the business. This methodology is spelled out in this book as a series of inter-related "patterns" for designing Internet-based business solutions. Several things are pos-sible when the workings of a company are coded on Internet web pages. First, the process becomes a tangible business artifact that is designed, built, and distributed just like any other supporting artifact the business makes or buys. Second, the process ceases to be something ephemeral, touchy-feely, ad-hoc, or something to be documented and then only referenced. Third, the business process comes alive on people's desktops in a way that gives business executives more options to adjust their company in response to the marketplace. Here are some examples:

- **Definition.** The process is defined as a set of granular procedural Web sites—one Web site for each business function that responds to a business event. The set of Web sites becomes the core business process. All business rules and operational data that each function needs is defined or referenced within its own process Web pages.
- **Design.** Process Web pages are distinctly separate from software applications. This means that the process is no longer designed into the applications. So, to change the way it operates, a company changes its Web pages, not its software ap-plications, a far easier task! This enables a company to more quickly adapt to business changes.
- **Implementation.** Process knowledge is built into all Web pages using colored hy-perlinks (e.g., blue for inputs, green for outputs, red for business rules). End users

can then personalize their browsers to use standard colors to help learn or remember the process, or to override the scheme.

- **Visibility.** As Web pages, the core business process is selectively opened (i.e., access is granted) or closed (i.e., access is denied) to any customer, channel, or supplier. This permits very fast implementation of high-level business decisions such as strategic alliances, mergers, acquisitions, customer acquisition, and outsourcing.

- **Deployment.** As Web pages, the process can be instantly placed on desktops to be read. This makes operations more consistent while reducing training costs. If portions of the process are given to a channel or supplier to carry out, Internet technology lets you monitor their operations and compute their performance in real time.

THE MIGRATION TO OPEN PROCESS

I expect this hidden value to be realized. The trend is already underway, albeit slowly, towards "open processes" for business. To say it a different way, the trend toward openness at the business process layer is being repeated just like the trend that led us to "open systems." We can explain the trend in this way. Back in the 1960s, mainframe computers were big, expensive to operate and maintain, and their hardware and software were proprietary. Then minicomputers arrived in the 1970s, followed by the personal computer and its clones in the 1980s. The 1990s saw computers become commodities, built with standard chips, operating systems, network connections, and so on. The kind of computing that allows us to "plug-and-play" we now commonly refer to as "open system."

The evolution that took computers to this state is now being repeated for processes. Today, the kind of process that is equivalent to the mainframe computer is called "enterprise resource planning" (ERP). This process (software) contains proprietary processes, and a business often alters its operations to accommodate those processes, similar to when mainframe computers were brought into a firm and all the manual procedures had to change. Internet-based processes are the process equivalent of "open systems." When designed and built in a particular way, they can plug-and-play and, thus, can be adapted more quickly than ERP systems. Open process frameworks is my way of conceptualizing those design principles that enable business processes to leap from proprietary to open.

Therefore, a hidden value of the Internet is its potential to make business processes tangible and, ultimately, into a commodity, so processes can be easily acquired and adapted. This can enable a firm to increase competitiveness within its marketplace, to link more intricately with its customers, to operate with far greater flexibility, and to respond more quickly to business events. Also, instead of spending large sums of money to purchase and install proprietary processes, a company can acquire a set of inexpensive Internet-based processes, and alter them to fit its operations. Since the business process is a set of Web pages, any portion of it can be selectively outsourced to sales channels, suppliers, distributors, and so on. This creates a distributed process platform that, because of how Internet technology works, can be remotely monitored.

BUSINESS ADAPTABILITY AND DURABILITY

From this perspective, corporate success in the 21st century will require using the Internet to maximize business adaptability and durability. To date, four strategies stand out. The first strategy is to make your company into an e-business organization (see Part I), one that takes full advantage of the Internet to achieve adaptability. The second is to create e-process architecture (see Part II) so that business processes can be rapidly developed, changed, outsourced, and insourced. The third is to develop a modular e-commerce platform (see Part III) that isolates the business, process, software, and data aspects of your company. The fourth is to realize e-project delivery (see Part IV) with a solid plan and senior team for implementing the e-business organization, e-process architecture, and e-commerce platform on scope, on time, and on budget. The figure below depicts the interrelationships among these four strategies, and how together, they create the adaptive e-enterprise.

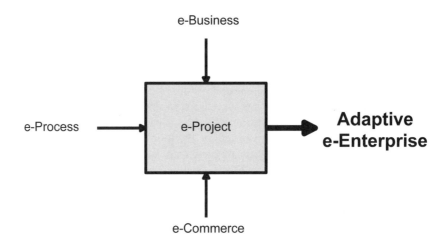

For three decades now, I have thought about, designed and implemented many process methodologies, actual business processes, and "open" solutions. I have also used the Internet from its earliest roots as the Arpanet to its current form. This book represents my best understanding of the combined potential of these subjects for business. It is a privilege to share this understanding with you, the reader. Since it took three decades to realize *Open Process Frameworks,* I hope the ideas presented herein will shorten the overall time it will take the business world to realize open processes and to transform businesses as we know them today into adaptive e-enterprises. In fact, this goal is why I founded my company, OpenProcess, Inc., back in 1997. My guess is that history will repeat itself, and in the end, how companies are designed, developed, and operated may change significantly because of the Internet, for the betterment of commerce in general.

DAVID A. MARCA
Newton, Massachusetts
October 27, 2004

ACKNOWLEDGMENTS

To Christopher Alexander, Sara Isikawa, Murray Silverstein, Max Jacobson, Ingrid Fiks-dahl-King, Shlomo Angel, and all the people who worked on the project to create "A Pattern Language." You gave the world its first hypertext book and a model for describing complex design as a series of patterns. I would not have been able to mentally formulate this book without your insight and guidance.

To Nancy Breen, Kevin Owens, Don Young, Tom Wilson, Gene Federowicz, Dave Smith, Jim Stellhorn, and Kerstin Dietz of Siemens Westinghouse Power Corporation for showing me world-class global contract labor outsourcing. To Sam Rossa, Bill Welch, Gary Hamlett, Hal Johnson, Frank Caserta, Peter Dennis, Bill Lage, Tom Young, and Meredith Humm of CDI Corporation for sharing their insights and knowledge of the staffing industry. To James Hawks, Meredith Humm, Dawn Pellar, Tom Manion, Anita Harding, and Margot Krismer for working with me on some of the best e-business solutions ever built for staffing.

To Bob Mannarino for mentoring me on business. To Jim Stellhorn and Beth Perdue for educating me on supply chain dynamics. To Doug Ross, Clare Feldman, Ken Schoman and Chuck Patrick for giving me the concept of "process." To Larry DeBoever, Corrine Brandi, and Beth Gold-Bernstein for introducing me to the concept of adaptability. To Russell Sutton for sharing his insights on vendor management technology. To Jack Bouvier for sharing with me his great wealth of knowledge on project management best practices. To all of the dedicated researchers and practitioners who designed and built the Internet.

To Clem McGowan, for being my steadfast colleague, mentor and guide during our almost 30-year careers in the commercial, military, and academic worlds. To Mike Albert, for his invaluable council during this project. To my review committee—Clem McGowan, Mike Albert, Jim Stellhorn, Dave Smith, Sam Rossa, Bill Welch, James Hawks, Mike Vannata, Jim Kilmurray, Matt Yuschik, Jim and Diane Morizio, and Ron Schaefer—for their enormously helpful direction on this project.

To my business coaches, Tricia Keene of TMI Executive Resources, and Marilyn Edelson of Ontrack Coaching and Consulting, Inc., who advised me on how best to complete this book. To Tom McNeil, Stuart Books, and Arthur Sullivan for their council at critical times in the life of my company, OpenProcess, Inc.

To my very good friends Mike Albert and Adam Kline for their steadfast support of me and my work. To my wife Julie and my daughter Kelsey for their love, motivation, and encouragement during the years it took to conceptualize this book, and during those long months of writing.

USING THIS BOOK

This book presents 16 conceptual frameworks, each comprising several design patterns for e-business, e-process, and e-commerce, plus project management anecdotes required for successful implementation. These patterns were written so that you can use them to design highly adaptable Internet-based solutions that support what we currently call "e-business" and all its underpinnings. Each pattern describes one key area of concern when designing e-business and e-commerce solutions.

For consistency, each pattern was given the same format. First, there is the pattern number and name, followed by an introductory paragraph. Its design principle is then given in italics, followed by a brief example of how the pattern is used. For this book, the running solution example is contract labor management. Lastly, a paragraph of design guidance is given, written so as to link the design pattern to others in the book.

From a conceptual viewpoint, when taken together, a set of patterns creates a framework. Each framework is introduced at the beginning of each chapter, followed by an explanatory figure and a narrative on how to interpret the figure. The patterns that create the framework are then presented, followed by a summary of the implications for using the patterns with the framework to develop solutions. This organization permits sequential reading of the patterns to see how they progressively build a framework.

This is not a hypertext book, so the sequence of patterns is linear. The particular chosen sequence starts with "business," because business context, mission, strategy, and plans all drive how a company must operate. The sequence continues with "process," because process defines how a company operates. Next in the sequence is "commerce," because it is the transactions themselves that realize the business and the process. The sequence ends with patterns found to be critical for successfully implementing the business–process–commerce patterns.

It is important to note that no pattern is an isolated entity. Each exists only to the extent that it is supported by the other patterns, not only those in its own framework, but those in other frameworks as well. The entire pattern collection can thus be thought of as a fundamental view of e-business, e-process, and e-commerce. This view says that you cannot build Internet-based solutions without considering the whole, the parts, and how the parts combine to form the whole. In other words, the act of design is a network of considerations that must be accounted for, and balanced.

Each chapter in the book contains a sequence of patterns, arranged as follows.

CHAPTER 1. BUSINESS ADAPTABILITY

Business adaptability is the speed at which a company can change itself to stay competitive. Internet technology enables competitiveness. If used to enable adaptability, it can also create business durability. The strategic importance of the Internet goes far beyond reengineering. It can implement every aspect of a company in a way that allows it to adapt to its ever-changing business environment. However, a company can organize itself in a particular way to take full advantage of the Internet. Chapter 1 describes the following open process patterns for creating an adaptable business:

1. Business Map
2. Internet Version of Your Business
3. Selectively Open and Close
4. Derived Performance and Savings Metrics
5. Open Internet-Based Business Processes
6. Highly Adaptable Technology Platform
7. Rapid "Go-to-Market" Strategy
8. Inject Standards into Operations
9. Dynamic Linking of Customers with Suppliers

CHAPTER 2. ENTERPRISE-WIDE SOLUTIONS

Chapter 1 uses general examples to present an open, adaptable framework for business competitiveness and durability. To understand the nuances of the remaining frameworks, a single running example of an Internet-based contract labor solution for large firms is used. Firms that use the Internet to place contract labor orders to a "supplier-neutral" pool are rethinking this solution. Those that outsourced their contract labor process to control supplier profits are examining their ROI. Their analyses are leading them to develop an enterprise-wide solution for better responsiveness and value generation:

10. Solutions to Tactical Problems
11. Standardize Key Locations
12. Enable Response to Change and Risk
13. Common Body of Knowledge
14. Leverage People and Information
15. Add Value to Suppliers

CHAPTER 3. MULTITIER SUPPLY CHAIN

Once the enterprise-wide solution has been conceptualized, the design of the contract labor management process can begin. The two most common designs are (a) supplier neutral and (b) process outsource. The former minimizes supplier profits, while the latter maximizes overall savings for the buying firm. Assuming that savings is your objective, a multitiered, outsourced supply chain process should be your goal:

16. Outsourced Process
17. Process Tiers
18. Master Agreement
19. Usage Directive
20. Flow-Down
21. Performance Metrics
22. Skill Niches
23. Standard Pricing Table
24. Supplier Subtiers

CHAPTER 4. INTERNET BUSINESS MODEL

Once the enterprise-wide solution has been conceptualized and a multitiered supply chain has been defined, an Internet business model is designed. The comprehensive model comprises a set of atomic e-business models, one for each link in the value chain. For each corporate entity, there are two links: the "sell-side" link and the "buy-side" link. For contract labor management, the Internet business model that yields the best savings is built using C2B on the "sell side" and B2V on the "buy side." The entire set of building blocks is:

25. Value Chain
26. Buy–Sell Process Alignment
27. Atomic e-Business Model
28. B2C Sell Direct
29. C2B Full Service
30. C2C Mediated Exchange
31. C2C Virtual Community
32. B2B Buy Direct
33. B2V Commodity Value

CHAPTER 5. ADAPTABLE TECHNOLOGY

Part I, e-Business, discussed the need for the entire company to think in terms of "adaptability." Mergers, acquisitions, business growth, cycle time reduction, alteration in customer demographics, and more are the forces driving companies to be highly flexible. Technology must, therefore, enable this kind of business flexibility. Fortunately, today's technology is not like its predecessor. Technology trends and convergence that occurred in the 1990s now make "adaptability" a possibility. But to capitalize on this requires a change in perspective:

34. Rethink "Technology"
35. Unlimited Storage
36. Inexpensive Computers

CHAPTER 6. INTERNET USAGE METAPHOR

Internet usage can take a form similar to media such as television, telephones, or encyclopedias. All these forms are valid, and each results in particular Internet solutions. However, by applying critical thinking, we can deduce that there is another basic way to view Internet usage—from a process point of view. From this fundamental perspective, the Internet is a process medium. As such, it enables the creation of highly adaptable Internet solutions that can be used to make an Internet Version of Your Business (2):

CHAPTER 7. INTERNET-BASED PROCESS

When each part of a business process can quickly make an e-business connection to a customer or a supplier, the adaptability of the business' operation is maximized. To achieve this goal, the process must: (a) be a set of integrated Web pages, (b) exhibit a consistent look and feel, and (c) point to specific software functions and detailed data elements for efficient running. The implementation must also produce files of live performance data, so the process can be monitored in real time:

CHAPTER 8. OPEN PROCESS ARCHITECTURE

One crucial factor for business durability discussed in Chapter 1 is a highly open process architecture. Since today's computing technology is adaptable, an open process architecture is now possible. However, adaptable process is not automatic; it must be very carefully designed. Fortunately, the design patterns are well known and come from the design of the Internet itself, and, prior to that, client/server computing:

55. Business Event
56. Business Response
57. Responses Share the Process
58. Network of Process Web Pages
59. Hyperlinks to Application GUIs
60. Hyperlinks to Web-based Forms
61. Application Logic Separate from GUI
62. Application Logic Separate from Data
63. Transactions Separate from Decisions

CHAPTER 9. BUSINESS ARCHITECTURE

Business architecture is now being recognized for its crucial role in addressing shrinking product life cycles, increasing competition, and individualizing customer needs. Especially for an e-Business, a firm must be highly adaptive. The term "turn on a dime" has been used many times to describe this ability, yet few can articulate what actually must be implemented to achieve high adaptability. At the business level, the key to operational adaptability is creating an organization that simultaneously permits autonomy, cooperation, and control among its business functions. The key to durability is to also maintain a very high degree of control over the evolution of all business functions:

64. Autonomous Business Functions
65. Cooperation via Event-Response Pairs
66. Control via Wholly Owned Business Rules
67. Control via Company-Wide Business Rules
68. Organizational Learning via Rule Revision

CHAPTER 10. PROCESS ARCHITECTURE

The number of variables that affect the corporate bottom line appears to be growing at an exponential rate, and one of those variables is the adaptable process. An adaptable and efficient process is essential for e-commerce because it enables a company to respond to its business events whenever and wherever they occur. Such a process is a network of autonomous functions that can dynamically connect themselves together via messages whenever a business event occurs:

69. Anywhere–Anytime Business Events
70. Respond at Point and Time of Event
71. Measurable Event–Response Pairs
72. Messages Implement Event–Response Pairs

73. Only Pass Messages to Respond to Events
74. Comprehensive Web Site for Each Function
75. All Needed Operating Rules on Each Web Site

CHAPTER 11. SOFTWARE ARCHITECTURE

Software applications must be able to immediately react to changes in the e-business or the e-process, and so they must be designed (prior to their construction) to be adaptable. Research suggests factoring ISO and object-oriented standards into software architectures in order to increase their adaptability. In addition to these standards, the following patterns, whose origins come from adaptable client/server technology, are suggested:

76. Physically Distinct Software Layers
77. Appropriate Use of Middleware and SQL
78. Separate GUI Event Handling from the GUI Logic
79. Separate Application Logic from Business Rules
80. Use Objects to Modularize the Data Access Logic
81. Separate Transactional Data from Reporting Data
82. All Reports Run Against the Data Warehouse
83. Reusable Procedures Written in XML, Java, or SQL

CHAPTER 12. DATA ARCHITECTURE

Without data, computers have no business purpose. It is the information asset that enables a business to correctly respond to its events. Database technology has a history of serving applications. First it served the applications that handle transactions, and then the applications that support decision making. Adaptable e-commerce applications place special requirements on how databases and data architecture should be used. As discussed in Chapter 11, these requirements center on the need to Separate Transactional Data from Reporting Data (81):

84. A Complete Event–Response = One Online Transaction
85. Business Functions Touch Only Transactional Databases
86. Isolate the Data Warehouse from Transactional Databases
87. Answer One Important Business Question First
88. Grow the Data Warehouse One Answer at a Time
89. Feed the Data Warehouse Automatically
90. Add Indexes to Speed up Trend Analyses

CHAPTER 13. MANAGEMENT FRAMEWORK

e-Business projects now absorb more of the IT budget, so firms are using disciplined programs to implement these initiatives, especially through enterprise project management.

e-Business project success requires balancing imagination and methodology while providing tight coordination among many the participating organizations to reduce risk. For
contract labor management, project timelines are often short and fixed, requirements
change must be controlled, project focus is on the outsourcing agreement, and implementation requires heavy coordination, single point of control, and external oversight. For
these reasons, an e-project relies heavily on a management framework:

91. Project Constraints and Assumptions
92. Solid Project Definition
93. Comprehensive Project Team
94. Accurate and Controlled Estimates
95. Tight Project Control
96. Project Repository
97. Proactive Project Oversight

CHAPTER 14. PROJECT MANAGEMENT

Some companies consider e-business initiatives to be very similar to traditional software
development efforts, so some e-business solutions are pressed into service with insufficient capability or usability. However, some companies recognize that e-business initiatives require more than the traditional planning, requirements, design, and testing activities common to other software efforts. They recognize that an e-project must use
management techniques from initiatives that have varying degrees of uncertainty and organizational impact—strategy implementations, for example. And because of the high
visibility and wide impact of an e-project, these companies also adopt structured and disciplined quality and learning methods to lessen project rework. In short, they institute five
additional key management practices:

98. Formal Project Stages
99. Highly Coordinated Project Team
100. Project Plan Management
101. Process Change Management
102. Technology Integration Management

CHAPTER 15. IMPLEMENTATION MANAGEMENT

Instituting a management framework and formal management practices will help alleviate
some common e-project mistakes, such as unsupportive champions, unclear strategy, conflicting priorities, and poor coordination. However, a comprehensive set of implementation practices is also needed to create a complete, correct, and usable e-business solution.
This includes all e-project communications:

103. Business Relationship Management
104. Commodity Pricing

CHAPTER 16. TEAM MANAGEMENT

Due its scope, complexity, and number of stakeholders, an e-project must take care to manage its relationships. These relationships span the sponsoring organization, the larger company, the value chain, and the user community. Therefore, the project team should employ a multiteam management approach and framework that enables customer focus, continuous improvement, total participation, and societal networking. It should also have subteams, each one capable of managing the relationship between the e-project and a specific constituency:

READING THE CASE STUDY

This is a book about designing the adaptive e-enterprise. As such, it is prescriptive in nature, highly organized, and has subject matter that is tightly linked via a web of interrelationships. It is therefore not a book that one would pick up and read like a novel. Instead, you absorb a pattern, see how the pattern relates to other patterns, and then see how several patterns can come together into a complete design.

By themselves, patterns are abstract and hard to grasp and use in everyday work. To bring them into a more usable form, a case study has been incorporated throughout this book. The example that is used for most patterns is a contract labor management solution. Appendix A describes this solution and gives a business rationale for why it was created. It was selected because it has the structure, depth, and nuance that typify an adaptive e-enterprise, yet it is not too large to grasp conceptually.

If you are not familiar with the staffing industry (i.e., the providing of contract labor), please read Appendix A before reading the rest of this book.

Each design pattern in this book has an example, and those examples are intended to be part of a larger solution. Appendix B is a set of excerpts from a real open process solution. Please read it before reading the rest of this book. It was written to show you what resulted when the patterns in this book were applied to build a contract labor management solution. For space considerations, only excerpts of the solution are given. The excerpts present the solution structure, how one accesses it from a computer, and what one sees (i.e., process, information, and function) from a Web browser.

The example in Appendix B is intended to give you a sense of a real open process, its form, structure, and salient attributes. An open process is (a) process implemented as a network of Web pages, (b) descriptions that can be understood and performed, (c) consistent process terminology and data names, (d) hyperlinks to live process data.

After reading both Appendix A and Appendix B, you are likely to find this book and the underlying design patterns of open process frameworks to be easier to read, relate to each other, and apply.

I

e-BUSINESS

To accomplish e-business—implementing a formal business relationship over open networks—factor the Internet across your entire company:

- Enable business adaptability (Chapter 1) by understanding how Internet technology can implement every aspect of your company in a way that allows it to adapt to business environment changes.
- Define an enterprise-wide solution (Chapter 2) by creating a map of your entire operation, and then use process outsourcing as a way to improve responsiveness and generate more business value.
- When outsourcing, design a multitier supply chain (Chapter 3) that not only generates response and value but generates additional savings without wasting effort trying to control supplier profits.
- Create one Internet business model (Chapter 4) to span all supply chains. Implement it with several atomic e-business models.

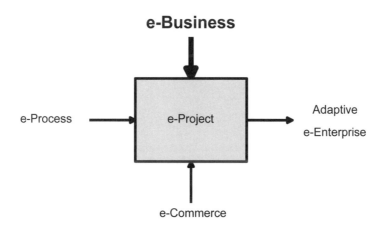

1

BUSINESS ADAPTABILITY

Business adaptability depends on the speed at which a company can change itself to stay competitive. Internet technology enables competitiveness. If used to enable adaptability,[19] it can also create business durability.[35] The strategic importance of the Internet goes far beyond reengineering.[1] It can implement every aspect of a company in a way that allows it to adapt to the ever-changing business environment.[17] However, a company can organize itself in a particular way to take full advantage of the Internet. These are the open process patterns for creating an adaptable business:

1. Business Map
2. Internet Version of Your Business
3. Selectively Open and Close
4. Derived Performance and Savings Metrics
5. Open Internet-Based Business Processes
6. Highly Adaptable Technology Platform
7. Rapid "Go-to-Market" Strategy
8. Inject Standards into Operations
9. Dynamic Linking of Customers with Suppliers

The resulting business organization would conceptually look like the one shown in Figure 1. A Business Map (1) is used to create an Internet Version of Your Business (2), and to then Selectively Open and Close (3) that business.

HOW TO INTERPRET FRAMEWORK #1

An adaptable business is organized into three distinct layers. The first layer is the result of strategic planning, tactical planning, and the execution of those plans. The overall business strategy and plan are developed, followed by the design of business operations and standards, followed by the design of key business information and partnerships. All these business elements are coded into Reusable Procedures Written in XML, Java, or SQL

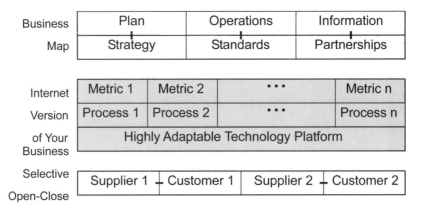

Figure 1   Framework #1. Business organization for high adaptability.

(83). This way, all business rules defined by senior management get immediately used and direct all business operations.

The second layer is the result of business process design or business process reengineering, and the design or adjustment of the technology infrastructure to support the business process. Process design is guided by operational requirements and standards. Metrics design is guided by the business plan and strategy. Technology design is guided not only by the metrics and processes, but also by the key business information and intercompany connectivity identified in the Business Map (1).

The third layer is the rapid selective opening and closing of the business process to customers and suppliers. This can happen only because the metrics, business process, and transactional systems are all implemented using Internet technology. This Internet Version of Your Business (2) is designed so that each and every element can potentially be accessed by any external party via the Internet. The actual opening and closing happens according to the partnerships defined in the Business Map (1).

These layers are created in the order given above. The Business Map (1) must completely define the business, how it is expected to operate, and how it is expected to connect to customers and other business, both now and in the future. Only with that comprehensive definition can the Internet Version of Your Business (2) be designed and implemented. Once implemented according to the patterns in this book, executives are free to adapt their company to the changes they perceive in the business environment, something they have never been able to do before.

The remainder of this chapter details each of the patterns that, together, create Framework #1.

Pattern 1. Business Map

Today, loss of market share, pricing power, or asset value[13,33] are causing companies to rethink how they use the Internet. Some are realigning themselves[16,30] in order to build an Internet version of their business from concept[29,34] to operation.[31] They begin by making a business map.[21,26,28,34]

Create a business map that unifies plans, operations, and information.

For example, an article in *Industry Week,*[2] stated that regardless of where you start e-procurement, it is imperative to look at your business process and the processes of your suppliers to come up with a single supply-chain process that you can use across multiple business units. End-to-end process design across the enterprise is a must.

Therefore, create a Business Map (1) that will enable you to Develop an Internet Version of Your Business (2) so that you can Selectively Open and Close (3) it to customers and suppliers.

Pattern 2. Internet Version of Your Business

Some companies are now rethinking, or have rethought, their use of the Internet to improve their competitive advantage. They understand that operational improvements do not necessarily translate into financial success.[25] These firms understand that Internet dynamics[19,32] will give them greater operational response,[20] efficiency,[14,24] and flexibility.[19]

> *Convert the business map into an Internet version of your business.*

For example, an article in *Technology Review*[3] reported that General Motors invested $1.7 billion in Internet applications while eliminating 3500 legacy systems. Now, car designs that took four years now take 21 months. The transition of internal operations to the Internet creates efficiencies.

Therefore, create an Internet Version of your Business (2) directly from the Business Map (1). Ensure that it contains Derived Performance and Savings Metrics (4), Open Internet-based Business Processes (5), and a Highly Adaptable Technology Platform (6).

Pattern 3. Selectively Open and Close

The Internet is an "open" technology[23]—any Internet application has the potential to be used by anyone with a Web browser. At every moment, therefore, corporate leaders have the option to open[18] (i.e., allow access to) any portion of their business, process, or Internet applications to one or more of the company's customers or suppliers.

> *Selectively open and close your business to customers and suppliers.*

For example, customers routinely now use their home Web browser to track their FedEx overnight packages. Similarly, consumers can send their custom automobile order directly to the manufacturing plant via an Internet application right in the Toyota car dealer showroom.

Therefore, ecide which customers and which suppliers will have access to which Internet applications. Continually decide how to Selectively Open and Close (3) to maximize competitive advantage.

Pattern 4. Derived Performance and Savings Metrics

Companies that rely on the Internet measure the effectiveness of their technology against their business plans. Performance metrics[15] such as "economic value added" (EVA)[4] and savings metrics such as "return on investment" (ROI) and "return on asset" (ROA) are common.

Derive performance and savings metrics from the business plan.

For example, an article in *Inc. Magazine*[5] described how PrintingForLess.com maximized the ROI of its printing presses by overbooking its online orders and using a database to automatically manage the backlog. New ways to manage order flow and production processes emerge when performance metrics become a design objective.

Therefore, create Derived Performance and Savings Metrics (4) to satisfy business plans. Put logic in the Open Internet-based Business Processes (5) to compute metric data. Display each metric on the Process Monitoring Dashboard (54).

Pattern 5. Open Internet-based Business Processes

When designed properly, one Web page can implement one process step. Taken together, these Web pages form an open Internet-based business process.[6] A highly adaptable business process has the ability to allow corporate leaders to make an "e-business partnership" at any point throughout the entire Internet-based business process.

Create open, Internet-based processes that support operations.

For example, an article in *BtoB Magazine*[7] reported that Wal-Mart, Inc. intends to move all of its supplier EDI transactions to the Internet in order to become a more "real-time" enterprise. The world-wide electronic commerce initiative is replacing proprietary networks with open networks.

Therefore, create a set of Open Internet-based Business Processes (5) that together implement an Adaptable e-Business Connection (46). Implement them on a Highly Adaptable Technology Platform (6).

Pattern 6. Highly Adaptable Technology Platform

The principles for adaptable Internet solutions are well known.[8] The resulting platform modularizes each business function.[27] Each maintains its own business rules and transactional data. Each function has its own highly reliable[36] hardware, database, and Internet applications.

Develop a highly adaptable technology platform to manage information.

For example, and article in *Inc. Magazine*[5] stated that Peppers and Rogers Group developed the now popular "Ask Albert" as its own Intranet to help its consultants locate reports, presentations, and notes. Sharing information, and organizing it so it can be shared, are two design goals.

Therefore, create a Highly Adaptable Technology Platform (6) using Customer Focused Technology (38). Implement it to be an Internet Business (45), so customers can view and touch core processes.

Pattern 7. Rapid "Go-to-Market" Strategy

Pioneering companies doing Internet commerce are creating business plans incrementally.[9] On each iteration, these companies add a new e-business building block[37] such as "direct to customer" and "full service provider." Each iteration increases their ability to go to market.

Quickly develop and adjust a "go-to-market" strategy to respond to business environment and market opportunities.

An article in *BtoB Magazine*[10] reported that Staples, Inc. managed to Internet-enable 80% of its largest customers, while driving online capabilities to about 70% of its total customer base. The Internet-enablement of the sales pipeline, including both customers and channels, is often a key part of an e-business strategy.

Therefore, create a Rapid "Go-to-Market" Strategy (7), then use a portion of the Internet Version of Your Business (2) to implement it. Inject Standards into Operations (8), then measure their effectiveness using Derived Performance and Savings Metrics (4).

Pattern 8. Inject Standards into Operations

The Internet version of a business is a set of Internet-based processes that, since they are implemented as software, can be quickly changed and immediately deployed across the enterprise. The next iteration of the "go to market" strategy determines what new standards must be implemented in order to achieve new customer–supplier partnerships.

Rapidly inject new standards into existing operations.

For example, an article in *Business Week*[11] stated that a large Wall Street firm helped Booze-Allen Hamilton, Inc. to combine four separate customer-relationship-management systems into one standard. The consolidation of sales history and trends so that data can assist in future decision making is often a key part of an e-business strategy.

Therefore, per the Rapid "Go-to-Market" Strategy (7), determine where to Inject Standards into Operations (8) in order to support Dynamic Linking of Customers with Suppliers (9). Achieve all-encompassing standards; avoid process variations.

Pattern 9. Dynamic Linking of Customers with Suppliers

An Internet version of a business is a dynamic portal that allows people to directly use the core processes of a company. The company is in total control of who actually sees and uses the core processes. When designed properly, the business result is a selective pairing of customer and supplier via the dynamic portal that adds value to both and generates revenue without no adding assets.

Dynamically link customers with suppliers to rapidly create new partnerships that add value.

An article in *Business Week*[12] reported that Panasonic, Inc. implemented an e-commerce system on IBM Websphere, and thus reduced its effort to connect specific customers with specific products. This is a business example of disintermediation; in this case, the removal of intermediate distributors to create efficiencies.

Therefore, per the Rapid "Go-to-Market" Strategy (7), Selectively Open and Close (3) the Internet Version of Your Business (2) so customer–supplier partnerships can view and touch core processes.

IMPLICATIONS OF PATTERN USE

Only if the Business Map (1) contains fully defined plans, operations, and information can the patterns of Rapid "Go-to-Market" strategy (7), Inject Standards into Operations (8), and Dynamic Linking of Customers with Suppliers (9) be accomplished.

The Highly Adaptable Technology Platform (6) must be put in place before the Internet Version of Your Business (2) can be constructed. Derived Performance and Savings metrics (4) should be generated for each major step in all Open Internet-based Business Processes (5). Metrics must be defined as early as possible in the e-project, because they are implemented for each tier in the resulting supply chain, and they may differ considerably from tier to tier or from supplier to supplier.

Once the Internet Version of Your Business (2) is developed from the Business Map (1), you can then decide how to Selectively Open and Close (3) it to customers, employees, and suppliers. Follow the plan for partnerships in the Business Map (1) to determine the sequencing of which customers, channels, and suppliers will see which portions of your business process and the scope of what they will actually see and touch.

REFERENCES

1. O'Brien, J. (2003). *Introduction to Information Systems.* McGraw-Hill Irwin.
2. Verespej, M. (2002). e-Procurement Explosion. *Industry Week,* March.
3. Rifkin, G. (2002). GM's Internet Overhaul. *Technology Review,* October.
4. Stewart, G. (1991). *The Quest for Value.* HarperCollins.
5. Cringely, R. (2002). Talking to the Tech Department. *Inc. Magazine,* December.
6. Marca, D. (2003). Software Engineering Experiences while Implementing Internet-based Business Processes. In *Proceedings of CCT'03,* August 2003.
7. Karpinski, R. (2002). Wal-Mart Pushes Web EDI. *BtoB Magazine,* October 14.
8. Gold-Bernstein, B. and Marca, D. (1997). *Designing Client/Server Systems.* Prentice-Hall.
9. Weill, P. and Vitale, M. (2001). *Place to Space: Migrating to e-Business Models.* Harvard Business School Press.
10. Karpinski, R. (2002). Web Delivers Big Results for Staples. *BtoB Magazine,* November 11.
11. Miller, R., Keenan, F., Palmeri, C., and Sager,I. (2002). The New Economy's New Austerity. *Business Week,* November 11.
12. Popper, M. (2002). A Tech-Spending Boom Ahead? *Business Week,* October 28.
13. Day, G. (1990). *Market Driven Value.* Free Press.
14. Korten, D. (1995). *When Corporations Rule the World.* Berrett-Koehler.
15. Osama, A. (2004). Creating Multi-Attribute Performance Measurement System for Sustaining High Performance. In *13th International Conference for the Management of Technology,* April 2004.
16. Rabaey, M. (2004). Aligning Business- and Resource-Strategy. In *13th International Conference for the Management of Technology,* April 2004.
17. Neblett, J. (2004). Environmental Factors Affecting a Firm's Ability to Compete. In *13th International Conference for the Management of Technology,* April 2004.

18. Ferguson, D., Sairamesh, J., and Feldman, S. (2004). Open Frameworks for Open Cities. *Communications of the ACM, 47,* 2, February.

19. Levene, M. and Poulovassilis, A. (2004). *Web Dynamics.* Springer-Verlag.

20. Adii, A., Botzer, D., Etzion, O., and Yatzkar-Haham, T. (2001). Monitoring Business Processes through Event Correlation Based on Dependency Model. In *Proceedings of the 2001 ACM SIGMOD Conference on Data Management,* Vol. 30, No. 2, May 2001.

21. Bernus, P., Nemes, L., and Schmidt, G. (2003). *Handbook of Enterprise Architecture.* Spinger-Verlag.

22. Phelps, S., Tamma, V., Wooldridge, M., and Dickinson, I. (2004). Toward Open Negotiation. *IEEE Internet Computing, 8,* 2, March–April.

23. Krovi, R., Chandra, A., and Rajagopalan, B. (2003). Information Flow Parameters for Managing Organizational Processes. *Communications of the ACM, 46,* 2, February.

24. Thrun, W. (2002). *Maximizing Profit: How to Measure the Impact of Manufacturing Decisions.* Productivity Press.

25. Looney, C., Jessup, L., and Valacich, J. (2004). Emerging Business Models for Mobile Brokerage Services. *Communications of the ACM, 47,* 6, June.

27. Anton, A., and Price, R. (2003). Functional Paleontology: The Evolution of User-Visible System Services. *IEEE Transactions on Software Engineering, 29,* 2, February.

28. Dalal, N., Kamath, M., Kolarik, W., and Sivaraman, E. (2004). Toward an Integrated Framework for Modeling Enterprise Processes. *Communications of the ACM, 47,* 3, March.

29. Cysneiros, L. and Leite, J. (2004). Nonfunctional Requirements: From Elicitation to Conceptual Models. *IEEE Transactions on Software Engineering, 30,* 5, May.

30. Casati, F., Shan, E., Dayal, U., and Shan, M. (2003). Business-Oriented Management of Web Services. *Communications of the ACM, 46,* 10, October.

31. Shanks, G., Tansley, E., and Weber, R. (2003). Using Ontology to Validate Conceptual Models. *Communications of the ACM, 46,* 10, October.

32. Singh, M. (2004). *The Practical Handbook of Internet Computing.* Chapman & Hall/CRC Press.

33. Fleming, Q. and Koppelman, J. (2004). *Earned Value.* Project Management Institute.

34. Go, K. and Carroll, J. (2004). The Blind Men and the Elephant: Views of Scenario-Based System Design. *Interactions, 11,* 6, November–December.

35. Malone, T., Laubacher, R., and Morton, M. (2003). *Inventing the Organizations of the 21st Century.* MIT Press.

36. Tian, J., Rudraraju, S., and Li, Z. (2004). Evaluating Web Software Reliability Based on Workload and Failure Data Extracted from Server Logs. *IEEE Transactions on Software Engineering, 30,* 11, November.

37. Linthicum, D. (2004). Twelve Steps to Implementing a Service Oriented Architecture. *B2B Community Library,* October.

2

ENTERPRISE-WIDE SOLUTIONS

Chapter 1 used general examples to present an open, adaptable framework for business competitiveness and durability. To understand the nuances of the remaining frameworks, a single running example of an Internet-based contract labor solution for large firms will be used. Firms that use the Internet to place contract labor orders to a "supplier neutral" pool[1] are rethinking this solution. Those that outsourced their contract labor process to control supplier profits are examining their ROI.[2] Their analyses are leading them to develop enterprise-wide solutions for better responsiveness and value generation. The patterns used to achieve this are:

10. Solutions to Tactical Problems
11. Standardize Key Locations
12. Enable Response to Change and Risk
13. Common Body of Knowledge
14. Leverage People and Information
15. Add Value to Suppliers

The resulting enterprise-wide solution would conceptually look like the one shown in Figure 2.1. The Common Body of Knowledge (13)—the memory about each Business Response (56) for each Business Event (55)—can Leverage People and Information (14) and Add Value to Suppliers (15).

HOW TO INTERPRET FRAMEWORK #2

An adaptable business has an enterprise-wide solution that is often layered into a hub-and-spoke configuration.

The first layer (the hub) is a set of operational policies. These policies often come about by solving key tactical issues facing the business. When produced from due diligence that considers the entire enterprise, these rules have utility across all business units and geographies. Therefore, they should be standardized into a Common Body of Knowledge (13) for use by all organizational entities and by all individuals.

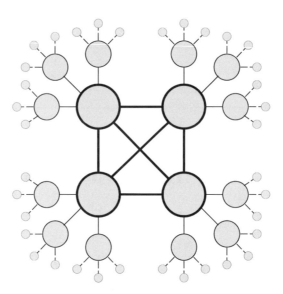

Figure 2. Framework #2: Internet technology distributes a common process.

The second layer (the main spokes) comprises the organizational entities of, and the individuals in, the business. The people, their departments, and the larger business units that manage departments must all decide to use the Common Body of Knowledge (13) to conduct business. When this happens, business rules Leverage People and Information (14) and have immediate and pervasive influence on how the business responds to its environment (i.e., how it responds to events, climate, industry shifts, regulations, competition, and so on).

The third layer (the secondary spokes) is the supplier community. On a day-to-day basis, suppliers interact with individuals. Since those individuals follow the same rules—because they are using the Common Body of Knowledge (13)—the business operates consistently and fairly with all its suppliers. As a last step, additional enterprise-wide rules should be created to Add Value to Suppliers (15) and to assist suppliers in helping them respond faster, with better quality, and at a reduced cost.

The hub-and-spoke framework is a well-know organizational architecture that permits the rapid dissemination of business rules. Arguments have been made that this structure is too hierarchic to be efficient and flexible. However, this notion has an underlying assumption—that the implementation of all aspects of the e-enterprise solution must follow this architecture. Internet technology gives us a new mechanism, whereby the rules can be hierarchically disseminated while the functions of the solution can be defined and operated in an autonomous manner. This gives us both control and flexibility. Achieving both requires solid design.

The remainder of this chapter details each of the patterns that, together, create Framework #2.

Pattern 10. Solutions to Tactical Problems

Traditional goals of controlling supplier profits are being examined against companies' needs to remain competitive.[10] If an e-Business solution can first solve all tactical concerns, then it frees up executives to solve the strategic concerns that ensures business durability.

> ***Make the first goal of the enterprise-wide solution to solve your business'***
> ***most pressing tactical problems.***

For example, the Internet-based solution must scale up and down[3] to the natural contract labor utilization cycles of the business (e.g., in spring and fall, power plants need extra maintenance staff) while providing real savings[12] on the contract labor used during "peak usage" periods.

Therefore, create Solutions to Tactical Problems (10) by focusing on the key business units of your company. Thoroughly conduct "due diligence" in order to solve all key tactical process-related problems at once.

Pattern 11. Standardize Key Locations

While solving the critical tactical problems, you will discover missing or ineffective policies and procedures.[4,18] An e-business solution relies on these policies and procedures to operate correctly. Due diligence identifies how to "shore up" key locations of the business to strengthen their operations.[11]

> ***Strengthen key locations by implementing new policies and procedures,***
> ***and standardize them across the enterprise.***

For example, a contract labor utilization directive is an often missing standard. This policy drives overall efficiency up by defining business situations in which contract labor use is appropriate and expected. Without such corporate-wide guidance, an e-enterprise initiative often fails.

Therefore, conduct thorough due diligence to identify missing policies and procedures, standardize them, and ensure that they become part of the Common Body of Knowledge (13). Inject Standards into Operations (8); do so before implementing the Internet Version of Your Business (2).

Pattern 12. Enable Response to Change and Risk

Standard operations are not enough, however.[5] Key locations must also know how to rapidly respond to changes in the business environment surrounding the company. They must also have risk mitigation and contingency policies, procedures, and information at their fingertips.

> ***Enable key locations to respond to change and risk with special policies,***
> ***procedures, and information.***

For example, some power plants have very old generators that require maintainers to have detailed knowledge of this equipment. An "on call" contract labor pool with such special skills is a risk contingency tool. So, upgrade the operating standards of key locations to Enable Response to Change and Risk (12). Add and highlight risk mitigation and contingency information in the Common Body of Knowledge (13). Also add special policies and procedures for rapid response to change.

Pattern 13. Common Body of Knowledge

An Internet-based content service[6] is the means by which standard policies and procedures for operations, and response to change and risk can be consistently and immediately deployed[14,16] throughout an enterprise. It enables a unified response to every business event.[15]

> *Create a common body of operational knowledge that everyone in your company will use to conduct business.*

For example, typical content in a body of knowledge[17] for an Internet-based contract labor solution would be: directive for contract labor usage, contract labor pricing policy, and requisition approval rules. Such rules often become the core of the standard operating procedures.

Therefore, compile all policies and procedures to Standardize Key Locations (11) and Enable Response to Change and Risk (12) into a Common Body of Knowledge (13). Make it accessible from every single Web page of the Internet Version of Your Business (2).

Pattern 14. Leverage People and Information

Leverage personnel into a hub-and-spoke design,[7] then disseminate the common policies and procedures of the key locations to this organization. This takes operational pressure off the enterprise.[8]

> *Couple the common body of knowledge with a hub-and-spoke organization to drive operational standards to everyone.*

For example, in large firms, local sites are required to follow contract labor management practices of their regional centers, but lack of formal lines of communication and common business rules most often result in frequent "rogue activity" in the requisition and hiring of labor. Therefore, Leverage People and Information (14) by creating a hub-and-spoke organization. Ensure that all locations use the Internet Version of Your Business (2) and follow the Common Body of Knowledge (13).

Pattern 15. Add Value to Suppliers

Once the hub-and-spoke organization is in place and supported by common business rules, the final organizational design element must address the value to be added to the supplier base. Proper design can reduce supplier costs and increase the value of supplier assets.[9]

> *Design a Enterprise-wide solution to reward the value of supplier assets and to simplify supplier efforts to fill orders.*

For example, an Internet-based contract labor solution automatically sends orders to suppliers via the Internet. This eliminates the cost of supplier sales activity. Also, orders are often sent based on supplier "skill niches." Thus, suppliers can assign specialists to fill these orders. Such use of the Internet creates efficiency in the back-end supply chain.

Therefore, Create Skill Niches (22) that will simplify supplier efforts to fill orders. Embed these niches into the Standard Pricing Table (23) and align the existing Supplier Subtiers (24) to the Skill Niches (22).

IMPLICATIONS OF PATTERN USE

Solutions to Tactical Problems (10) must be implemented first, and must be placed in those locations from which they can best be replicated and distributed. Allow for tightly controlled configurations due to location specifics. Once all are identified, Standardize Key Locations (11).

Key locations are subsequently bolstered with organizational knowledge to Enable Response to Change and Risk (12). Once proven to be effective, that organizational knowledge is placed in the Common Body of Knowledge (13). This repository thus becomes the corporate memory about each Business Response (56) to each Business Event (55).

Once built, the Common Body of Knowledge (13) can be used to Leverage People and Information (14) to achieve faster response to business events and better company-wide problem solving. It can also be used to Add Value to Suppliers (15), to simplify their processes, and to enable them to potentially improve the extent of their participation.

REFERENCES

1. Ariba, Inc. (2004). B2B Marketplaces in the New Economy. Ariba White Paper. (URL: http://www.ariba.com/).
2. Group, R. (2004). Working Effectively with Standard Outsourcing Contracts. Bitpipe Featured Report. B2B Community Library Annex. (URL: http://www.bitpipe.com/), February 2004.
3. Weill, P. and Vitale, M. (2001). *Place to Space: Migrating to e-Business Models.* Harvard Business School Press.
4. Dalal, N., Kamath, M., Kolarik, W., and Sivaraman, E. (2004). Toward an Integrated Framework for Modeling Enterprise Processes. *Communications of the ACM, 47,* 3, March.
5. Joyce, W., Nohria, N., and Roberson, B. (2003). *What (Really) Works: The 4+2 Formula for Sustained Business Success.* Harper Collins.
6. Ferguson, D., Sairamesh, J., and Feldman, S. (2004). Open Frameworks for Information Cities. *Communications of the ACM, 47,* 2, February.
7. Hammer, M. (2001). *The Agenda: What Every Business Must Do to Dominate the Decade.* Crown.
8. Prior, M. (2002). Streamline the Supply Chain. *DSN Retailing Today, 41,* 5, March.
9. Dawar, N. and Vandenbosch, M. (2004). The Seller's Hidden Advantage. *MIT Sloan Management Review, 45,* 2, Winter.
10. Biehl, B. (1995). *Stop Setting Goals—If You Would Rather Solve Problems.* Ballantine.
11. Burack, E. and Torda, F. (1979). *The Manager's Guide to Change.* Lifetime Learning Publications.
12. Krauter, E. (2004). Profitsharing and Gainsharing Programs and Their Influence on Productivity. In *13th International Conference for the Management of Technology,* April 2004.
13. Schulz, W. and Hofer, C. (2004). Creating Value through Skill-Based Strategy and Entrepreneurial Leadership. In *13th International Conference for the Management of Technology,* April 2004.

14. Stuckenschmidt, H. and Van Harmelen, F. (2004). *Information Sharing on the Semantic Web.* Springer-Verlag.

15. Cleland-Hang, J., Chang, C., and Christensen, M. (2003). Event-Based Traceability for Managing Evolutionary Change. *IEEE Transactions on Software Engineering, 29,* 9, September.

16. CFF Project Team. (2000). A Framework for Collaborative Computing. *IEEE Internet Computing, 4,* 1, January–February.

17. Singh, M. (2004). *The Practical Handbook of Internet Computing.* Chapman & Hall Publishers/CRC Press.

18. Malone, T., Crowston, K. and Herman, G. (2003). *Organizing Business Knowledge. The MIT Process Handbook.* MIT Press.

3

MULTI-TIER SUPPLY CHAIN

Once the enterprise-wide solution has been conceptualized, the design of the contract labor management process can begin. The two most common designs are (a) supplier neutral[1] and (b) process outsource.[2] The former minimizes supplier profits, whereas the latter maximizes overall savings for the buying firm. Assuming that savings[14] is your objective, a multitiered, outsourced supply chain process should be your goal. The patterns are:

16. Outsourced Process
17. Process Tiers
18. Master Agreement
19. Usage Directive
20. Flow-Down
21. Performance Metrics
22. Skill Niches
23. Standard Pricing Table
24. Supplier Subtiers

The resulting supply chain organization would conceptually look like the one in Figure 3. Note the Flow-Down (20) of the Master Agreement (18).

HOW TO INTERPRET FRAMEWORK #3

An adaptable business has one or more supply chains whose processes are designed using both the business map and enterprise-wide solution. The first tier comprises the business itself, with its Common Body of Knowledge (13) that is shared across all business units, departments, and individuals. The important thing to accomplish is to create strong standards at this point in the overall solution to enable much more flexibility and decentralization across the rest of the supply chain.[18] These rules are "packaged" into Master Agreements (18), one agreement for each required supply chain. Each master agreement defines

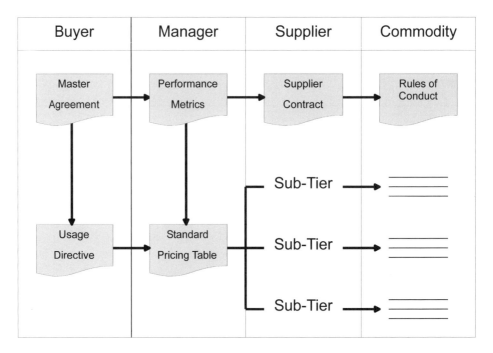

Figure 3.1. Framework #3: The managing entity directs the supply chain.

the operational objectives for its supply chain, as well as the rules comprising the commodity Usage Directive (19).

The second tier is the process manager for the supply chain. This entity can be inside the business, or it can be a third party; the latter results from an Outsourced Process (16). The managing entity is responsible for the Performance Metrics (21) and compliance rules for the supply base. A key compliance standard is the Standard Pricing Table (23). The definition of performance and compliance is done through the Flow-Down (20) of Master Agreement (18) provisions into supplier subcontracts.

The third tier comprises the supplier community. Each supplier agrees to a subcontract, which appropriately models the Master Agreement (18). Sometimes, commodity characteristics, business needs, business cycles, or geographic scope create situations that constrain commodity provisioning. In these cases, the supplier community can be partitioned into Supplier Subtiers (24), each of which has unique rules to enable commodity fulfillment inside the constraints created by the business.

The fourth tier is the commodity itself. This tier appears when the commodity must perform to business, industry or regulatory standards. For example, in the case of contract labor, the rules for how people are to conduct themselves while working on the business' premises are a key element in determining how well the overall commodity (i.e., people in this case) are utilized. This concept can be generalized by considering how a commodity should be used by operations in order to respond to business events as fast and as well as possible.

The remainder of this chapter details each of the patterns that, together, create Framework #3.

Pattern 16. Outsourced Process

Outsourcing begins with the decision to make a single firm responsible for undertaking the role of digital intermediary.[3] This company becomes not only the control point, but the solution owner.[16] Its process and technology, especially its Internet applications,[15] must create an end-to-end value chain that links all suppliers and consumers.[3]

> *Designate one firm as the sole owner of the entire process.*

For example, an outsourced contract labor management process is successful when the outsourcing company designates one firm to own the process, creates a contract defining the role, communicates the decision to the supplier base, and supports the firm in that role.

Therefore, create an Outsourced Process (16) by assigning the entire role to one firm. Require a Program Office Team (115) to act as control point, and create a Master Agreement (18) to govern its actions.

Pattern 17. Process Tiers

The owner of the outsourced process is far more than just a distributor. The firm adds value with its knowledge[4] of enterprise-wide order patterns and mix, fulfillment trends, and labor pool availability across the supply base. The optimal way to gain this knowledge while controlling the end-to-end process is to create a tiered process.

> *Create a tiered process that enables knowledge acquisition as well as control. Distinguish order, fulfillment, and commodity.*

For example, process tiers isolate rules, procedures and transactions for each entity in the supply chain: buyer, supplier, and commodity. This simplifies the control of, and knowledge acquisition about, each entity. Such a design creates new opportunities for supplier participation.

Therefore, create Process Tiers (17) to isolate the operating rules for each major entity from the others. Use Performance Metrics (21) to acquire knowledge about each entity's operating trends and patterns.

Pattern 18. Master Agreement

The process outsource is made formal with a contract. This document establishes a master electronic trading partnership agreement[5] with the outsourcing company and the service firm responsible for the process.

> *Create a master service agreement that defines the outsourced process and all the expectations for the process owner.*

For example, the master service agreement defines contract terms and conditions such as process boundary, geographic coverage, scope of functional responsibility, and expected performance and savings. But good contracts do not overconstrain; for example, they let the new process owner define the flow-down terms to the supplier base.

Therefore, create a Master Agreement (18) that defines the process, process ownership, and the expected savings. Put the Performance Metrics (4) and a Standard Pricing Table (23) in the contract.

Pattern 19. Usage Directive

Most companies assume that a contract is enough to ensure success.[12] However, experience has shown that well-defined rules are required to avoid difficulty in implementing the contract labor solution.[6] These rules also make possible the enforcement of buyer and supplier compliance.[17]

> *Publish a clear and concise contract labor usage directive that defines*
> *roles, authority, demand, requisition, duration, and conduct.*

For example, a directive defines (a) business conditions that trigger use of contract labor, (b) limits of authority for both contracting parties, (c) assignment duration limits, (d) preapproved exceptions for requisitions, and (e) required manager conduct to minimize risk to the company. The directive often becomes the overarching business rule for operations.

Therefore, write a Usage Directive (19) that is specifically designed to Inject Standards into Operations (8). Tie it to the Rapid "Go-to-Market" Strategy (7). Make it part of the Common Body of Knowledge (13).

Pattern 20. Flow-Down

The master agreement must define the nature of the work of all parties by taking into account the tiered approach.[7] In other words, not all terms in the contract apply to every process tier. Thus, the owner of the outsourced process must "flow-down" contractual terms appropriately.

> *Create subcontracts for each process tier. Decide which master agreement*
> *terms apply to each. Define them so they can be measured.*

For example, pricing is a master agreement term that applies to the supplier tier but not to the commodity tier. However, rules for completing and submitting a time card apply to both the supplier and commodity tiers. Therefore, a designer of an e-enterprise must take care to pinpoint the target tier for each contractual term and condition.

Therefore, Flow Down (20) terms in the Master Agreement (18) to the Process Tiers (17) so that each party understands how to operate. Ensure that operational definitions align with the Performance Metrics (21).

Pattern 21. Performance Metrics

Contracts without measures often yield poor results. Experience shows that a measurement methodology, integrating bottom-up and top-down performance metrics, is an effective approach.[8] Measurement that is balanced across the entire outsourced process yields optimal results.

***Create a balanced set of performance metrics that span both the
outsourced process and the tiers within the process.***

For example, (a) a buyer metric can quantify the situations causing labor demand, (b) a
process owner metric can show savings by quarter, and (c) a supplier metric can plot satisfaction onto assignment cost and duration. Thus, a set of metrics can measure the entire
e-enterprise solution.

Therefore, create a small set of Performance Metrics (21) for each of the Process Tiers
(17). Measure all key subcontract terms and all key expected rules of conduct. Ensure
that, as a group, they generate the Derived Performance and Savings Metrics (4) for the
business plan.

Pattern 22. Skill Niches

An outsourced process often has a large scope—the demand of the outsourcing company
is large and no one supplier can satisfy it. Wise suppliers know there is value in specialization.[9] They can participate, distinguish themselves from their competition, and make a
profit.

***Allow contract labor suppliers to define their "skill niches" to give them
control of competitive positioning and profits.***

For example, one supplier may choose to participate by supplying most of the required
labor at a low price due to the high volume involved, whereas another supplier may
choose to participate by providing just one "rare" skill that commands a high price. Electronic auctions are common in this setting. Such use of the Internet gives suppliers more
freedom to select how and where they wish to participate in the overall e-enterprise solution.

Therefore, Add Value to Suppliers (15) by permitting Skill Niches (22). Ensure that all
suppliers participate within the constraints of the Standard Pricing Table (23). Provide the
same Flow-Down (20) to all suppliers.

Pattern 23. Standard Pricing Table

Standard pricing benefits the buyer because it generates savings by constraining price.
But it also benefits suppliers. The combination of a fixed price with a guaranteed order
stream levels the playing field by minimizing extra costs (e.g., sales), especially to small-
er suppliers.[10]

Define a commodity pricing standard that generates overall savings.

For example, labor price standardization involves identifying anomalies (i.e., prices
much higher than market), defining benchmarks[13] (i.e., price alignment to those typical in
the company's industry), identifying price elasticity (i.e., high volume creates below-mar-
ket price opportunity). The result is a tool that controls spending while enabling faster
pricing changes.

Therefore, create a Standard Pricing Table (23) that generates overall savings without
impeding the rapid "go-to-market" strategy. Measure its performance with Derived Per-

formance and Savings Metrics (4). Make it comprehensive so it can Add Value to Suppliers (15).

Pattern 24. Supplier Subtiers

Examination of the supplier base may indicate that a "flat" supplier tier is not optimal. In some cases, just a few suppliers can provide most of the commodities within the buying demand pattern (first subtier), whereas all others provide just specific value-added contributions (second subtier).[11]

> *Create supplier subtiers if you discover that only a few suppliers satisfy a high percentage of the overall demand.*

For example, some Fortune 100 companies create a first subtier that provides most of the contract engineering skills, and a second subtier that provides very specialized, but infrequently used, engineering skills. Such a design optimizes the fulfillment of a large percentage of the labor, while also enabling better fulfillment on hard to acquire skill sets.

Therefore, under certain circumstances, create Supplier Subtiers (24) to simplify the operations and the management of the Outsourced Process (16). Flow Down (20) the Master Agreement (18) to all subtiers. Apply Performance Metrics (21) equally across all subtiers.

IMPLICATIONS OF PATTERN USE

Remember to create strong standards in the solution to enable much more flexibility and decentralization across the rest of the supply chain. The two most common solution designs are supplier neutral and process outsource. The former, low-end solution supports transactions (i.e., the so-called "self-service" transactions), whereas the latter, high-end solution provides a comprehensive service (i.e., the so-called "full service" transactions).

The Outsourced Process (16) solution can be optimal, especially if a master service provider can be found to implement it at no direct cost. (This is common for contract labor outsourcing solutions.) Implementing this solution requires a Master Agreement (18) that defines distinct Process Tiers (17), and defines Flow-Down (20) terms and conditions for the Supplier Subtiers (24). It is from the latter that supplier Performance Metrics (21) are derived. These metrics monitor supplier operations and also their cost, thereby mitigating cost build-up lower down in the chain.

The two key governing documents for the e-business solution are the Usage Directive (19), which constrains the order process, and the Standard Pricing Table (23), which spans all Skill Niches (22), which constrain the fulfillment process (thus providing operational equity).

REFERENCES

1. Byungjoon Y., Choudhary, V., and Mukhopadhyay, T. (2002). A Model of Neutral B2B Intermediaries. *Journal of Management Information Systems, 19,* 3, March.
2. Enhanced Service Generates Profits. *Marketing* (UK), March 2003.

3. Griffin, D. and Halpin, E,. (2002) Local Government: A Digital Intermediary for the Information Age? *International Journal of Government & Democracy in the Information Age, 7,* 4, April.

4. Sinclair, R. (2003). Focusing on the Big Three.. *Electronics Weekly,* 2114, September 10.

5. Dan A. (2001). Business-to-Business Integration with tpaML and a Business-to-Business Protocol Framework. *IBM Systems Journal, 40,* 1, January.

6. Concerning the Strengthening of Labor Contract Management and the Improvement of the Labor Contract System. *Chinese Law & Government, 34,* 1, January/February, 2001.

7. Rubery, J., Earnshaw, J., Marchington, M., Cooke, F., and Vincent, S. (2002). Changing Organizational Forms and the Employment Relationship. *Journal of Management Studies, 39,* 5, July.

8. Bullinger, H., Kühner, M., and Van Hoof, A. (2002). Analysing Supply Chain Performance Using a Balanced Measurement Method. *International Journal of Production Research, 40,* 15, October 15.

9. Stoffer, H. (2003). Supplier Group Touts Greener World. *Automotive News, 78,* 6057, September 15.

10. Adshead, A. (2003). Web EDI Forces Suppliers to Change Tactics. *Computer Weekly,* July 1.

11. Doran, D. and Roome, R. (2003). An Evaluation of Value-Transfer Within a Modular Supply Chain. *Proceedings of the Institution of Mechanical Engineers Journal of Auto Engineering, 217,* 7, July.

12. Posner, K. (1995). *The Leadership Challenge.* Jossey-Bass.

13. Spendolini, M. (1992). *The Benchmarking Book.* American Management Association.

14. Krauter, E. (2004). Profitsharing and Gainsharing Programs and Their Influence on Productivity. In *13th International Conference for the Management of Technology,* April 2004.

15. Gasos, J. and Thoben, K. (2003). *E-Business Applications.* Springer-Verlag.

16. Tas, J. and Sunder, S. (2004). Financial Services Business Process Outsourcing. *Communications of the ACM, 47,* 5, May.

17. Basili, V., Shull, F., and Lanubile, F. (1999). Building Knowledge through Families of Experiments. *IEEE Transactions on Software Engineering, 25,* 4, July–August.

18. Malone, T. (2004). *The Future of Work: How the New Order of Business Will Shape Your Organization, Your Management Style, and Your Life.* Harvard Business School Press.

4

INTERNET BUSINESS MODEL

Once the enterprise-wide solution has been conceptualized and a multitiered supply chain has been defined, an Internet business model is designed. The comprehensive model comprises a set of atomic e-business models,[1] one for each link in the value chain.[2] For each corporate entity, there are two links: the "sell side" link, and the "buy side" link. For contract labor management, the Internet business model that yields the best savings[15] is built using C2B on the "sell side" and B2V on the "buy side." The entire set of building blocks is:

25. Value Chain
26. Buy–Sell Process Alignment
27. Atomic e-Business Model
28. B2C Sell Direct
29. C2B Full Service
30. C2C Mediated Exchange
31. C2C Virtual Community
32. B2B Buy Direct
33. B2V Commodity Value

The resulting Internet business model would conceptually look like the one in Figure 4. Notice that two, not one, atomic e-business models are used to implement a complete, end-to-end Internet business model.

HOW TO INTERPRET FRAMEWORK #4

An adaptable business has an Internet business model that comprises two, not one, atomic e-business models.

A business is not an isolated entity. It has customers and suppliers. Therefore, a business should be thought of in supply chain terms. It is, in effect, a Value Chain (25) comprising two links: a "sell side" link (i.e., how it interacts with its customers), and a "buy side" link (i.e., how it interacts with its suppliers). Each link is, therefore, implemented with one atomic e-business model, and the models may be quite different from each other.

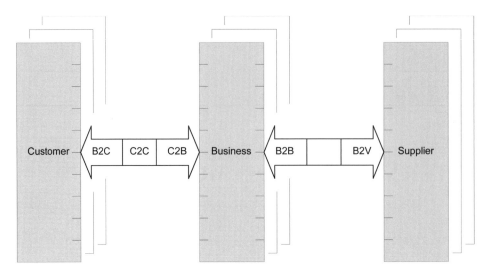

Figure 4. Framework #4: Two atomic e-business models per company.

Three different atomic e-business models are possible for the sell-side link. The B2C Sell Direct Model (28) positions a business as an entity from which customers buy products directly. The C2B Full Service Model (29) positions a business as an entity that provides some kind of value beyond just products. The C2C Mediated Exchange (30) positions a business as a broker between buyers and sellers. The C2C Virtual Community Model (31) can be used in conjunction with the other models to enable customers to talk to each other before buying.

Two different atomic e-business models are possible for the buy-side link. The B2B Buy Direct Model (32) positions a business as an entity that buys commodity directly from each supplier. The B2V Commodity Value Model (33) positions a business into being an entity which, for some reason (e.g., volume, unique need, business scope), can command some kind of value from a supply base. Full implementation happens when the buy-side link is coupled with the sell-side link.

Today, people naturally think of a business as being either B2C or B2B. this thinking is natural when the concept that the business participates in a supply chain is missing. Additional value, operational possibilities, and efficiencies can be created when a value chain perspective is used to assess how the e-enterprise should be constructed. Also, adaptability is increased when Internet connectivity of a business to its customers and suppliers is defined to be "atomic" in nature, rather than overarching in nature. The modularization of Internet-based connections is a powerful tool for executives to create anywhere–anytime business connectivity.

The remainder of this chapter details each of the patterns that, together, create Framework #4.

Pattern 25. Value Chain

In a value chain,[4] a company is viewed as a set of basic activities that add value to offerings and improve margin. Some activities are part of the core process and some support it.

An Internet-based value chain efficiently[16] implements not only the company's processes, but also its relationships with customers and suppliers.[2,6]

> *Use the Internet to implement strategic and tactical relationships with customers, channels, and suppliers throughout the entire value chain.*

For example, when FedEx let its customers "touch" its core process, allowing them to see real-time package tracking status, it strengthened customer relationships and improved its image and customer trust.[9] This design became a model for what we now call "opening the core process."

Therefore, view each Outsourced Process (16) as a Value Chain (25). Create links between the Process Tiers (17) in the chain, and use an Atomic e-Business Model (27) to forge each link.

Pattern 26. Buy–Sell Process Alignment

Research has shown that buyers typically go through the following mental process: need, search, select, buy, satisfy, and loyalty.[3] Success comes when a firm's process supports each step in the buyer process: identify need, buyer focus, competitive advantage, value proposition, service, and reward.[3] The processes must align.

> *Each link in the value chain is a business relationship. Define each as a buy-sell process. Ensure the sell process aligns with the buy process.*

For example, usability studies[17] of Reebok's first Web site showed that customers had difficulty searching for shoes. Reebok redesigned its entire Web site to ensure that each customer would need only three clicks to get to the shoe they wanted, regardless of where they were in the Web site.

Therefore, give each link in the Value Chain (25) its own process. Use the buyer's mental process to create Buy–Sell Process Alignment (26).

Pattern 27. Atomic e-Business Model

The way any one value chain link operates may differ from all the other links. So, to maximize adaptability, a company should consider modular implementation—each link is one of a standard set of buy–sell "building blocks." We refer to these as atomic e-business models.[1]

> *Implement each buy–sell process using standard building blocks called "atomic e-business models."*

For example, for contract labor management, experience shows that overall savings are maximized when the "sell" link is implemented with C2B Full Service (29), in which one supplier manages the whole endeavor, and the "buy" link is implemented with B2V Commodity Value (33).

Therefore, choose one Atomic e-Business Model (27) for the "sell" link and one for the "buy" link of a Value Chain (25). Make sure each model implements the expected Buy–Sell Process Alignment (26).

Pattern 28. B2C Sell Direct

The business-to-customer (B2C) model is the electronic equivalent of retail.[7,20] The goal is to have customers buy directly from you. Some of the key objectives are: offer lower price, bypass other suppliers, increase geographical area without increasing infrastructure, and distinguish value based on a set of objective measures.[1]

> *Use a B2C atomic e-business model if your objective is to implement a value chain link under a retail scenario.*

For example, B2C addresses back-end efficiency, market expansion, inventory management, cost reduction, and customer service benefits.[7] Contract labor management would not benefit from this model, as sales still occur, management activity remains, and labor cost is not reduced.

Therefore, choose B2C Sell Direct (28) when your objective is to create a retail relationship with your customers. This model will require a sales investment similar to traditional retail (e.g., banner ads[8]).

Pattern 29. C2B Full Service

The customer-to-business (C2B) model produces a value-added buying environment[19] to reduce operational costs and create a personalized buying process.[10,18] One supplier, the intermediary,[20] owns the primary customer relationship and, thus, is expected to meet all buyer needs in one URL. Integrating all offerings via a select set of third parties[1] is common.

> *Use a C2B atomic e-business model if your objective is to create a highly personalized, value-added buying environment.*

For example, an outsourced contract labor management process is a prime example of this atomic model. The managed service provider must reduce labor costs while also taking over many of the labor management activities. Internet technology is the best tool for doing this economically.

Therefore, choose C2B Full Service (29) when you intend to reduce operational costs and commodity costs. Let the full-service provider decide how to implement the "sell side" link of the Value Chain (25)

Pattern 30. C2C Mediated Exchange

The customer-to-customer (C2C) mediated exchange model creates one URL to connect buyers and sellers by concentrating information on providers, products, and services.[1] Properly classified, this knowledge simplifies searching and selecting. The model also mediates buying.[11]

> *Use a C2C mediated exchange atomic e-business model if your objective is to add value with information and mediation.*

For example, C2C mediators can be portals (e.g., Yahoo!), electronic malls (e.g., iMall), shopping agents (e.g., Jango), electronic markets (e.g., NASDAQ), and electronic auctions (e.g., eBay).[1] They all rely on large buyer and supplier bases, strong brands, and large assortments.

Therefore, choose C2C Mediated Exchange (30) when information and buying process management can create competitive advantages, especially if surveillance of buying activities helps achieve regulatory compliance.

Pattern 31. C2C Virtual Community

The customer-to-customer (C2C) virtual community model is the last vestige of the original Internet. It creates a single URL that builds an online community[12] around a common interest, thus bringing together buyers and sellers, and generating returns as the community grows.[1]

> *Use a C2C virtual community atomic e-business model if you can build a highly valued online community around a common interest.*

For example, many e-commerce sites now have some kind of "chat room" to grow the buyer community. Customer segmentation, new membership, governance, and sustainability are all key considerations when designing that portion of the e-enterprise that supports customers.

Therefore, use C2C Virtual Community (31) in the Value Chain (25), where buyer communication can support the success of other Atomic e-Business Model (27) building blocks in the Internet business model.

Pattern 32. B2B Buy Direct

The business-to-business (B2B) model helps a firm organize supplier offerings according to its areas of interest (to simplify selection), and discount them for volume purchases.[1] Suppliers are challenged with large the amount of variation needed to satisfy multiple businesses.[13,20]

> *Use a B2B atomic e-business model if your objective is to create a reliable, specialized commodity stream.*

For example, a single point of access for a particular area of interest can greatly simplify buyer operations. Some Web sites now allow individuals and companies to create their own "my_.com" for customizing offerings and streamlining ordering. Thus, the e-enterprise designer must think through how to enable customization inside the fixed business rules.

Therefore, use B2B Buy Direct (32) if one or a few suppliers can provide most of a particular commodity, but do not overburden the suppliers by requiring high maintenance to satisfy your business' special interests.

Pattern 33. B2V Commodity Value

The business-to-group (B2V) model establishes a competitive supplier base. The goal is to acquire commodities having best freshness, quality, price, assortment, or personalization.[3] Unlike B2B, it creates one portal and removes the need for ad hoc or proprietary integrations.[14]

Use a B2V atomic e-business model if your objective is to create a reliable stream of better-than-average market commodity value.

For example, the owner of an outsourced contract labor process can use this atomic model to provide that labor at prices that often beat market rates. When implemented properly, B2V creates a context in which suppliers are measured on both responsiveness and cost.

Therefore, use B2B Commodity Value (33) to improve a commodity stream. Create a Standard Pricing Table (23) to achieve better cost. Use Performance Metrics (21) to measure the improvement.

IMPLICATIONS OF PATTERN USE

An Adaptable e-Business Connection (46) always has "sell side" and "buy side" links in its Value Chain (25). Optimal transactions occur when each link has Buy–Sell Process Alignment (26). One Atomic e-Business Model (27) is used to implement each link. So, an Adaptable e-Business Connection (46) is implemented with two, not one, atomic models:

- The "sell side" atomic models are B2C Sell Direct (28), C2B Full Service (29), C2C Mediated Exchange (30), and C2C Virtual Community (31). Some contract labor solutions rely on the C2C model to support auction-like transactions. However, some firms are now migrating to the C2B model to optimize overall cost and control of their contract labor.
- The "buy side" atomic models are B2B Buy Direct (32) and B2V Commodity Value (33). The B2V model is optimal for contract labor outsourcing solutions because it supports consistent pricing across a commodity type while being sensitive to pricing differences due to commodity niches.

Preserving the distinction between "sell side" and "buy side" will always simplify design and implementation. Using one Atomic e-Business Model (27) for each "side" gives designers options for how to make each connection. Also, if additional "sell side" or "buy side" connections are required, a different atomic e-business model can be used without destroying the integrity of the original design, a property that is absolutely essential for creating an adaptive e-enterprise.

REFERENCES

1. Weill, P. and Vitale, M. (2001). *Place to Space: Migrating to e-Business Models.* Harvard Business School Press.
2. Nickerson, R. (2001). *Information Systems: A Management Perspective.* McGraw-Hill Irwin.
3. Rayport and Jaworski. (2004). *Introduction to Electronic Commerce.* McGraw-Hill Irwin.
4. Porter, M. and Millar, V. (1985). How Information Gives You Competitive Advantage. *Harvard Business Review,* July–August.
5. Reebok, Inc. (2004). Reebok store. (URL: http://store.reebok.com/ home/index.jsp).

6. Robeiro, F. and Love, P. (2003). Value Creation Through an e-Business Strategy: Implication for SMEs in Construction. *Construction Innovation, 3,* 1, March.

7. Youlong Z. and Lederer, A. (2003). An Instrument for Measuring the Business Benefits of E-Commerce Retailing. *International Journal of Electronic Commerce, 7,* 3, Spring.

8. Lohtia, R., Donthu, N., and Hershberger, E. (2003). The Impact of Content and Design Elements on Banner Advertising Click-through Rates. *Journal of Advertising Research, 43,* 4, December.

9. Ildemaro, A. and Iván, A. (2003). Developing Trust in Internet Commerce. In *2003 Conference of the Centre for Advanced Studies Conference on Collaborative Research,* October 2003.

10. Liliana, L., Anna, G., Giovanna, P., and Marino S. (2002). The Adaptive Web: Personalization in Business-to-Customer Interaction. *Communications of the ACM, 45,* 5, May.

11. Insights and Analyses of Online Auctions. *Communications of the ACM, 44,* 11, November.

12. Friesen, G. (2004). Redefining B2C From "Business to Consumer" to "Building Toward Community." *Consulting to Management—C2M, 15,* 1, March.

13. Ariel, F., Paolo, G., Manuel, K., and John, M. (2001). Information Systems as Social Structures. In *International Conference on Formal Ontology in Information Systems,* Vol. 2001, October 2001.

14. Asuman D., Yusuf T., Pinar P., Sait P., Gokce L., Gokhan K., Serkan T., and Yildiray K. (2002). Beyond Relational Tables. In *2002 ACM International Conference on Management of Data,* June 2002.

15. Krauter, E. (2004). Profitsharing and Gainsharing Programs and Their Influence on Productivity. In *13th International Conference for the Management of Technology,* April 2004.

16. Krovi, R., Chandra, A., and Rajagopalan, B. (2003). Information Flow Parameters for Managing Organizational Processes. *Communications of the ACM, 46,* 2, February.

17. Johnson, J. (2004). Web Bloopers: Common Web Design Mistakes and How to Avoid Them. In *ACM Professional Development Seminar,* October 23, 2004.

18. Miller, B., Konstan, J., and Riel, J. (2004). PocketLens: Towards a Personal Recommender System. *ACM Transactions on Information Systems, 22,* 3, July.

19. Lightner, N. (2004). Evaluating e-Commerce Functionality with a Focus on Service. *Communications of the ACM, 47,* 10, October.

20. Kotler, P. (1999). *Kotler on Marketing: How to Create, Win and Dominate Markets.* Free Press.

II

e-PROCESS

To accomplish the e-process—completing business processes over open networks—implement it so it can be selectively opened and closed:

- Think of the Internet as an adaptable technology (Chapter 5). Then, create an event–response technology platform designed to be customer focused while being able to adapt to business changes.
- Fully consider the underlying Internet usage metaphor (Chapter 6) to determine (a) how users will perceive and use your solution, and (b) the solution type—online business or Internet business.
- Design the solution as an Internet-based process (Chapter 7) so it can establish an e-business connection to a customer or a supplier without any additional design or implementation.
- Utilize an open process architecture (Chapter 8) to separate business events, the process, the applications, and the data.

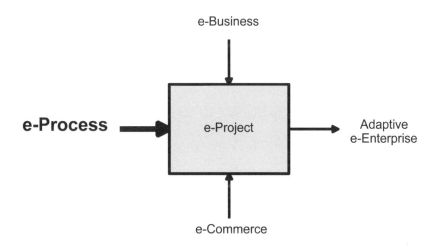

5

ADAPTABLE TECHNOLOGY

Part I, e-Business, discussed the need for the entire company to think in terms of "adaptability." Mergers, acquisitions, business growth, cycle time reduction, alteration in customer demographics, and more are the forces driving companies to be highly flexible. Technology must, therefore, enable this kind of business flexibility. Fortunately, today's technology is not like its predecessor. Technology trends and convergence that occurred in the 1990s now make "adaptability" a possibility. But to capitalize on this requires a change in perspective. The patterns that accomplish this are:

34. Rethink "Technology"
35. Unlimited Storage
36. Inexpensive Computers
37. Instantaneous Networks
38. Customer-Focused Technology

The resulting Internet technology layering would conceptually look like that in Figure 5. This organization is a Customer-Focused Technology (38)[21] solution that implements the "sell side" link of a Value Chain (25).

HOW TO INTERPRET FRAMEWORK #5

Achieving business adaptability and durability in the 21st century requires executives to Rethink "Technology" (34). Unlimited Storage (35), Inexpensive Computers (36), and Instantaneous Networks (37) should be aggressively combined to shift a company into being a high-performing, event-response machine. For some firms, this involves a fundamental shift in perspective on how to use technology. However, this perspective must also be balanced with a business perspective, one that sees the Internet as a Customer-Focused Technology (38).

Customer Focused Technology (38) has four layers. The first layer is the Internet portal for a company, where customers buy via a standard or personalized portal, and where they may talk with other customers before they buy. The second layer is the extranet por-

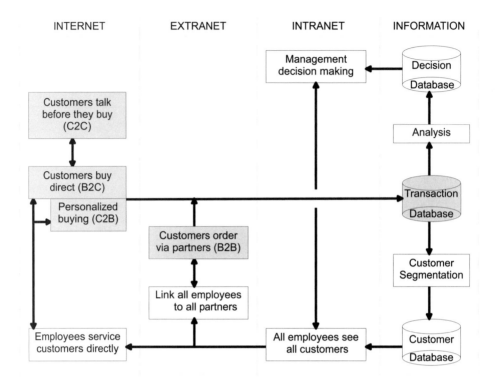

Figure 5. Framework #5: Internet technology for atomic e-business models (adapted from reference 9).

tal, where channels assist customers in their buying. The third layer is the intranet portal, where management and employees cooperate to make the company succeed. The fourth layer houses the company's key databases—one that enables transactions, one that remembers transactions for decision making, and one that remembers customers.

The remainder of this chapter details each of the patterns that, together, create Framework #5.

Pattern 34. Rethink "Technology"

There is a business value of technology.[1] Technology participates in operations, decision making, and strategy formulation for competitive advantage. When designed and implemented to match the structure and operation of a company, technology becomes that company.

> *Computers are not just computation devices; they are the embodiment of your business. Therefore, apply Internet technology everywhere.*

For example, some CEOs report that there is no distinction in their minds between a business initiative and an information technology initiative.[2] Some are issuing directives to digitize or outsource every function that does not directly touch the customer.[1] Especially with the Internet, how a business implements its strategic plan is intimately tied to technology.

Therefore, Rethink "Technology" (34) by understanding how Unlimited Storage (35), Inexpensive Computers (36), and Instantaneous Networks (37) can create competitive advantages. Create layers of increasing business "openness" with intranet, extranet, and Internet portals.[22]

Pattern 35. Unlimited Storage

Information storage capacity, reliability, and performance are increasing at three times the rate of the last century.[3] Database replication is now common for world-wide applications,[4] and databases that automatically adjust themselves to get better performance are now available.[5]

> *Save every transaction, interaction with the customer, and business decision. Within the constraints of security and privacy policies, let all employees see all this data to make more informed decisions.*

For example, Sears Roebuck[10] increased warrantee sales by giving customer data to each service technician. Once an appliance is repaired in a home, the owner is far more likely to buy a warranty than when purchasing that same appliance in the store.

Therefore, use Unlimited Storage (35) to put information at employees' fingertips. Let each Business Response (56) own its operational data.

Pattern 36. Inexpensive Computers

Computer processors, the chips inside the boxes, are increasing their speed 100 times per decade, and today's personal computers now contain one or more of these extremely fast processors.[6] With these enormous speed increases has also come enormous cost decreases.

> *Use a computer whenever and wherever it is needed. Do not try to maximize processor utilization. Run one line of software logic on one computer if that will yield the best business solution.*

For example, Brigham & Women's Hospital[11] dedicates one computer to running just one business rule: "Watch all admissions computers and check for a former patient returning within 24 hours." On that event, a lawyer is beeped to speak with the person to ensure that there has been no malpractice.

Therefore, put Inexpensive Computers (36) everywhere they need to be, dedicate them to specific Business Response (56) functions, and tie them all together with Instantaneous Networks (37).

Pattern 37. Instantaneous Networks

Today's Internet backbone[1] is made of fiber optic cable. Many Internet service providers and companies use fiber. The remainder use "T1" lines as their network infrastructure.

Also, today's network software enables very high data throughput rates and network utilization.[7]

> ***Do not constrain a solution by physical proximity of its elements. Assume (but verify!) that the total network will be fast enough to handle all needed information exchanges between all elements.***

For example, Progressive Insurance[12] put its claim agents in cars having laptops networked by satellite. These agents go to the scene of an accident, or to the insured person's work or home, to settle claims. Within roughly 30 minutes, the car owner is issued a settlement check.

Therefore, put all employees where they physically need to be, and deliver the information they need via Instantaneous Networks (37).

Pattern 38. Customer Focused Technology

The driver of world economic growth has shifted from manufacturing volume to customer value.[8] Business durability now requires a company to constantly reorganize itself[16] to generate customer value and loyalty. Internet technology can implement that new organization.[9]

> ***Create layers of information processing and visibility that support conducting business as a single, integrated, and customer-focused activity. Use different Internet technology for each layer.***

For example, extranet portals[13,17] can support channels[18] while they create orders with customers. Intranet portals[14,17] can send real-time data to separate teams as they collaborate on new products. Internet portals[15,17] can offer personalized products based on prior purchases.[19] This concept of "layers of Internet technology" helps business executives think through high-level decisions about how to implement their strategy.

Therefore, create varying degrees of business "openness" with intranet, extranet, and Internet portals. Where appropriate, implement a portal with an Atomic e-Business Model (27).

IMPLICATIONS OF PATTERN USE

Companies that only have deep knowledge and experience in legacy applications or client/server technology must Rethink "Technology" (34) in order to understand the potential value of the Internet.

Unlimited Storage (35) allows a company to respond to a business event at the time the customer has a need to purchase. Inexpensive Computers (36) allow a company to dedicate as many computers as necessary to run software applications so that the response to every business event is as fast as it needs to be. Instantaneous Networks (37) allow a company to respond to a business event at, or very near to, the place where the event took place.

Customer-Focused Technology (38) is a careful blend of Unlimited Storage (35), Inexpensive Computers (36), Instantaneous Networks (37), and the latest Internet technologies (i.e., Internet, extranet, and intranet "portals") to achieve both an appropriate level of rapid response[20] and thorough, real-time support for both customers and channels.

REFERENCES

1. Nickerson, R. (2001). *Information Systems: A Management Perspective.* McGraw-Hill Irwin.

2. Radcliff, D. (2000). Aligning Marriott. *Computerworld,* April 20.

3. Gibson, G. (1995). Redundant Arrays of Inexpensive, Independent Disks (RAID) and Beyond. In *ACM SIGMOD International Conference on Data Management,* Vol. 24, No. 2, February 1995.

4. Petersen, K., Spreitzer, M., Terry, D., and Theimer, M. (1996). Replicated Database Services for World-wide Applications. In *Proceedings of the 7th ACM SIGOPS European Workshop,* September 1996.

5. Arpaci-Dusseau, R. (2003). Run-time Adaptation in River. *ACM Transactions on Computer Systems, 21,* 1, February.

6. Barton, M. and Withers, G. (1989). Computing Performance as a Function of the Speed, Quantity, and Cost of the Processors. In *1989 ACM-IEEE Supercomputing Conference,* August 1989.

7. Bethel, W., Tierney, B., Lee, J., Gunter, D., and Lau, S. (2000). Using High Speed WANs and Network Data Caches to Enable Remote and Distributed Visualization. In *ACM-IEEE Supercomputing Conference,* November 2000.

8. Cronin, M. (1996). *The Internet Strategy Handbook.* Harvard Business School Press.

9. Seybold, P. and Marshak, R. (1998). *How to Create Profitable Business Strategy for the Internet and Beyond.* Times Books.

10. Weigel, D. and Cao, B. (1999). Applying GIS and OR Techniques to Solve Sears Technician-Dispatching and Home-Delivery Problems. *Interfaces, 29,* 1, January–February.

11. Davenport, T. and Glaser, J. (2002) Just-in-Time Delivery Comes to Knowledge Management. *Harvard Business Review, 80,* 7, July.

12. Slywotzky, A. and Wise, R. (2003). Growing Pains. *Marketing Management, 12,* 3, May.

13. Ling, R. R. and Yen, D. C. (2001). Extranet: A new wave of Internet. *S.A.M. Advanced Management Journal, 66,* 2, Spring.

14. McNay, H. (2000). Communication and Learning. Corporate Intranets: Building Communities with Data. In *Proceedings of IEEE Professional Communication Society International Professional Communication Conference,* September 2000.

15. Beck, M., Moore, T., Abrahamsson, L., Achouiantz, C., and Johansson, P. (2001). Enabling Full Service Surrogates Using the Portable Channel Representation. In *Proceedings of the 10th International Conference on the World Wide Web,* April 2001.

16. Rangarajan, S., Phoha, V., Balagani, K., Selmic, R., and Iyengar, S. (2004). Adaptive Neural Network Clustering of Web Users. *IEEE Computer, 37,* 4, April.

17. Bellas, F. (2004). Standards for Second-Generation Portals. *IEEE Internet Computing, 8,* 2, March–April.

18. Lee, Y., Lee, Z., and Larsen, K. (2003). Coping With Internet Channel Conflict. *Communications of the ACM, 46,* 7, July.

19. Miller, B., Konstan, J., and Riel, J. (2004). PocketLens: Towards a Personal Recommender System. *ACM Transactions on Information Systems, 22,* 3, July.

20. Patterson, D. (2004). Latency Lags Bandwidth. *Communications of the ACM, 47,* 10, October.

21. Lightner, N. (2004). Evaluating e-Commerce Functionality with a Focus on Customer Service. *Communications of the ACM, 47,* 10, October.

22. Smith, M. (2004).Portals: Toward an Application Framework for Interoperability. *Communications of the ACM, 47,* 10, October.

6

INTERNET USAGE METAPHOR

Internet usage can take forms similar to media such as television, telephones, or encyclopedias. All these forms are valid, and each results in particular Internet solutions. However, by applying critical thinking,[33] we can deduce that there is another basic way to view Internet usage—from a process point of view. From this fundamental perspective,[1,2,3] the Internet is a process medium. As such, it enables the creation of highly adaptable Internet solutions that can be used to make an Internet Version of Your Business (2):

39. Fundamental Assumptions
40. Internet as Television
41. Internet as Telephone
42. Internet as Encyclopedia
43. Internet as Process
44. Online Business
45. Internet Business

The ways of visualizing the Internet as different kinds of media are shown in Figure 6. Thinking of the Internet as a process medium would emphasize "work," "collaboration," and "openness."

HOW TO INTERPRET FRAMEWORK #6

The Internet is a new medium, and as such, each of us has a personal bias about it and how it should be used. This bias is formed by our Fundamental Assumptions (39) about the media we already know: television, telephones, and encyclopedias. The Internet as Television (40) bias emphasizes advertising and traditional selling and buying. The Internet as Telephone (41) bias emphasizes conversations and information exchanges. The Internet as Encyclopedia (42) bias emphasizes content and searching. There is nothing wrong with any of these biases. They simply shape what is possible.

To complicate matters, these biases have gone unexamined since the Internet first came into widespread use. In addition, these biases are often intermingled, and thus often complicate one's understanding and one's use of Web sites. For example, one can often

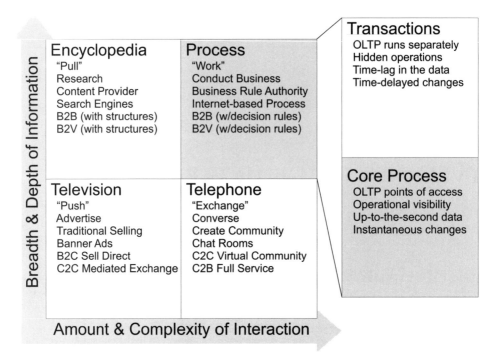

Figure 6. Framework #6: "Internet as Process" enables process adaptability.

see the Internet as Television (40) bias—banner ads—immediately adjacent to an Internet as Telephone (41) bias—the chat room. Typically, banner ads create such a distraction that online conversation is often interrupted, which causes either confusion or misinterpretation by one or both conversing parties.

Therefore, one goal of this framework is to distinguish the Internet usage metaphors for e-enterprise designers so they are better equipped to design capability, behavior, and appearance that consistently makes sense to end users. Whenever a transition between metaphors must occur, the user should be well aware of what is taking place. The second goal of this framework is to enable the Internet to be used in a new way—to create open processes. A new bias creates new possibilities.

The Internet as Process (43) bias emphasizes conducting work according to a set of well-defined rules. This leads to two different kinds of Internet usage approaches. The first approach is to use the Internet to build an Online Business (44) in which operations are hidden from customers and there are time delays in transactions and reporting data. The second approach is to use the Internet to build an Internet Business (45) in which operations are visible to customers, transactions complete "instantly," and reporting data is as close as possible to being instantaneous.

The remainder of this chapter details each of the patterns that, together, create Framework #6.

Pattern 39. Fundamental Assumptions

Atomic e-business models did not materialize in a vacuum. They came about because people have strong fundamental assumptions[1,2,3] about what the Internet is and how it is used. Typically, we do not examine our perspectives[1] on, biases[2] toward, and decisions[3] we make about media we use.

> *Be very aware of the fundamental assumptions about media that you bring to the design and implementation of Internet solutions.*

For example, we initially understand a new medium by trying to relate it to our experiences and decisions about existing media. Go back into the television archives to the very first TV programs. They show people physically gathered around microphones reading scripts. They were conducting TV broadcasts as if they were on radio! People's deep-rooted assumptions about radio were driving their very early use of television.

Therefore, deeply examine your Fundamental Assumptions (39)—your biases—about television, telephones, and written reference materials before starting a project to implement an Internet solution.

Pattern 40. Internet as Television

Viewed as television, the Internet is awash with online advertising, with annual growth projected at over 20%.[4] Banner ads,[5] content-centered e-mail,[6] and webcasts[7] are today's Internet ads. But to be successful in Internet advertising, understanding the factors for these kinds of media is crucial.[8]

> *To support B2C sell direct and C2C mediated exchange models, employ successful advertising practices found on TV and radio.*

For example, the clicking of a banner ad depends on several factors: (a) level of product involvement, (b) congruency between the content of a vehicle and the product category of the banner ad, (c) attitude toward the vehicle, and (d) overall attitude toward web advertising.[9] Especially in creating brand awareness, this Internet usage metaphor has utility.

Therefore, if your goal is to use the Internet as Television (40), create capabilities such as visually stunning Web pages, online catalogs and brochures, and banner ads and e-mail rewards that are "pushed" to customers.

Pattern 41. Internet as Telephone

Viewed as a telephone, the Internet is filled with conversations[10] that occur in online settings such as chat rooms[11] (originally called bulletin board systems[11]), e-mail-based inquiry systems,[13] and electronic conferencing systems15 for online discussion groups[16,18] and end-user forums.[20]

> *To support C2B full service and C2C virtual community models, design both the intended conversations and their online support.*

For example, online inquiries may be followed up with a phone call,[14] online discussions create additional email,[17] esoteric acronyms may arise,[11] regulating information flow helps focus online forums,[12] and social dynamics occur within a virtual community,[19] including selfcorrection.[16] The practice of explicitly designing conversations before they occur[35] can greatly improve this kind of Internet usage.

Therefore, if your goal is to use the Internet as Telephone (41), create capabilities such as online inquiries, bulletin boards, chat rooms, and electronic conferencing for discussion groups or end user forums. Design them to support the kinds of conversations you want to take plac.

Pattern 42. Internet as Encyclopedia

Viewed as an encyclopedia, the Internet is an information network. As a digital archive,[23,24] its accuracy and reliability[27] are highly variable, its content is sometimes difficult to read,[22,23], and searching it can be difficult.[26] In other words, the vastness of Internet as an information repository makes accessing it according to one's intentions very difficult.

> *To support B2B buy direct and B2V commodity value models, design a
> digital archive that is overengineered for easy searching.*

For example, people often only visit the first three results of their online search, spending 60 seconds or less at each.[25] Due to time pressures, people create oversimplistic queries, succeeding only half the time.[26] Catalog lists[22] and table of contents[22] have been used as effective aids.

Therefore, if your goal is to use the Internet as Encyclopedia (42), create a trusted, digital archive of products, documentation, and upgrades. Overdesign its structure to enable easy reading and searching. Obtain the person's underlying intent for the search prior to creating the search algorithm. Put data no further than three mouse clicks from the home page.

Pattern 43. Internet as Process

Viewed as a process, the Internet is a sea of e-business connections.[28] When each part of a business process can quickly make an e-business connection to a customer or supplier, the operational aspect of that business has been maximized to its highest level of adaptability.[31]

> *To support B2B buy direct or B2V commodity value atomic e-business
> models, create a process-oriented e-business connection between the firms.*

For example, software engineering and adaptable technology principles are central to adaptable e-business connections.[29,30] Also, it has been shown that once a process is modularized to the level of one Web page per process step, it can then be turned into an e-business connection.[31] Current methods for business process design are very applicable here.

Therefore, if your goal is to use the Internet as Process (43), then define your business as a sequence of process steps, define each step and its rules as a Web page, and then decide how to further implement each: (a) manually, (b) as a specific Internet application, or (c) outsourced to a supplier.

Pattern 44. Online Business

Today, many Internet solutions are of the "online" category[34] because e-commerce is transactional (i.e., not procedural) in nature.[31] In the end, customers are kept from viewing, and interacting with, the online transaction processing (OLTP) system that runs a firm's operations.

> ***Create an online business if your competitive advantage is not at risk if customers and suppliers cannot "touch" the core process.***

For example, Boston Fleet Bank's Homelink application lets you do ATM transactions and bill paying from your browser. However, account balances are not updated until the next business day, just like an ATM. In this case, for both business and technology reasons, the bank decided not to allow their customers to change account data in real time.

Therefore, if your goal is to create an Online Business (44), create Internet solutions that implement time-delayed information exchanges, such as those that result from the perspectives of: Internet as Television (40), Internet as Telephone (41), and Internet as Encyclopedia (42).

Pattern 45. Internet Business

An Internet business[32] exists when both customers and suppliers are allowed to view or interact with the online transaction processing (OLTP) system that runs a firm's operations. Here, the end user follows the same procedural rules as anyone employed by the company.[31]

> ***Create an Internet business if your competitive advantage is at risk if customers and suppliers cannot "touch" the core process.***

For example, Security First National's Internet banking application lets you do ATM transactions and bill paying from your browser. However, unlike an ATM, your account balances are immediately updated. This design puts the customers in direct contact with their accounts. There is no buffering between transaction and result. Many of the difficulties and errors people experience in their bank accounts is due to the buffering banks create. This is why customers really like Security First National's system.

Therefore, if your goal is to create an Internet Business (45), employ the Internet as Process (43) perspective to create Internet solutions that implement real-time business conversations, business operations, and business transactions based on up-to-the-second live data.

IMPLICATIONS OF PATTERN USAGE

People have strong (and often unexamined) Fundamental Assumptions (39) about what the Internet is, and what an Internet solution can do.

Internet as Television (40) is based on the assumption that the Internet is a visual medium. Internet as Telephone (41) is based on the assumption that the Internet is a conversational medium. Internet as Encyclopedia (42) is based on the assumption that the Internet is an informational medium. Internet as Process (43) is the assumption that the Internet is a network of business-to-business connections, each governed by business rules and process.

An Adaptable e-Business Connection (46) typically has a strong bias toward one of the above Fundamental Assumptions (39). It also has a strong bias to it being either an Online Business (44) that has time-delayed information exchanges and no access to the core business process, or an Internet Business (45) that has real-time information exchanges with full access to the core business process.

Every adaptable business connection has an underlying bias. A bias is not "right" or "wrong." A bias simply limits how one thinks about customers, channels, products, services, suppliers, and so on, as well as what kind of Adaptable e-Business Connection (46) should be built. Make sure you identify the underlying bias for your solution so that you can assess whether or not it is the most effective one for your business purpose.

REFERENCES

1. Senge, P. (1990). *The Fifth Discipline.* Doubleday.
2. Burke, J. (1985). *The Day the Universe Changed.* Little, Brown.
3. Kuhn, T. (1970). *The Structure of Scientific Revolutions.* University of Chicago Press.
4. Lamar, B. (2003). Web Ads Get a Move On. *Advertising Age, 74,* 44.
5. Battelle, J. (2003). Putting Online Ads in Context. *Business 2.0, 4,* 5, May.
6. Sernovitz, A. (2003). Content-Centered E-mail in 6 Steps. *B to B Magazine, 88,* 12, December.
7. Maddox, K. (2003). Marketers Demand Effective Measures. *B to B Magazine, 88,* 5, May.
8. Baltas, G. (2003). Determinants of Internet Advertising Effectiveness: An Empirical Study. *International Journal of Market Research, 45,* 4, December.
9. Cho, C. (2003). Factors Influencing Clicking of Banner Ads on the WWW. *CyberPsychology & Behavior, 6,* 2, February.
10. Levine, R., Locke, C., Searls, D., and Weinberger, D. (1999). *The Cluetrain Manifesto: The end of business as usual.* Perseus Books.
11. Munro, J. (2003). EZ Interaction. *PC Magazine, 22,* 23.
12. Carnegie, T. (2003). Teaching a Critical Understanding of Virtual Environments. *Business Communication Quarterly, 66,* 4.
13. An Open Source Dozen. (2003). *Library Journal,* Net Connect, *128, 12,* December.
14. Schriener, J. (2003). Talking the Old-Fashioned Way. *Engineering News-Record, 251,* 16.
15. Angeli, C., Valanides, N., and Bonk, C. (2003). Communication in a Web-based Conferencing System: The Quality of Computer-Mediated Interactions. *British Journal of Educational Technology, 34,* 1.
16. Anonymous. (2004). Using Group Work to Promote Community, Sharing Expertise. *Online Classroom,* March.
17. Minkel, W. (2004). You've Got Too Much Mail. *School Library Journal, 50,* 2, February.
18. Anonymous (2004). A Guide to Discussing "Ill-Structured Problems" Online. *Online Classroom,* February.
19. Schrock, D, Holden, D., and Reid, L. (2004). Creating Emotional Resonance: Interpersonal Emotion Work and Motivational Framing in a Transgender Community. *Social Problems, 51,* 1, January.
20. Reich, G. (2004). Internet Event Examines Use of Topas® COC in Design and Manufacturing. *Medical Design Technology, 8,* 1, January.
21. Descy, D. (2004). Searching the Web: From the Visible to the Invisible. *TechTrends. 48,* 1, January.

22. Hauer, M. and Simedy, W. (2002). intelligentCAPTURE 1.0 Adds Tables of Content to Library Catalogues and Improves Retrieval. *Information Services & Use, 22,* 4, April.

23. Artemis Images. (2003). Providing Content in the Digital Age. *Entrepreneurship: Theory & Practice, 28,* 2, February.

24. Panos, P. (2003). The Internet Archive: An End to the Digital Dark Age. *Journal of Social Work Education, 39,* 2, February.

25. Thilmany, J. (2003). Web Searchers Measure Site's Appeal in Seconds. *Mechanical Engineering, 125,* 10, October.

26. Meyer, P. (2003). Net Search Engines: How Good Are They? *Business & Economic Review, 50,* 1, January.

27. Tatsioni, A., Gerasi, E., Charitidou, E., Simou, N., Mavreas, V., and Loannidis, J. (2003). Important Drug Safety Information on the Internet: Assessing its Accuracy and Reliability. *Drug Safety, 26,* 7, July.

28. Ragins, E. and Greco, A. (2003). Customer Relationship Management and E-Business: More Than a Software Solution. *Review of Business, 24,* 1, January.

29. Zwass, V. (2003). Electronic Commerce and Organizational Innovation: Aspects and Opportunities. *International Journal of Electronic Commerce, 7,* 3, March.

30. Zhu, K. and Kraemer, K. (2002). e-Commerce Metrics for Net-Enhanced Organizations: Assessing the Value of e-Commerce to Firm Performance in the Manufacturing Sector. *Information Systems Research, 13,* 3, March.

31. Marca, D. (2003). Software Engineering Experiences While Implementing Internet-based Business Processes. In *Proceedings of CCT'03,* August 2003.

32. Souitaris, V. (2004). Internet Business or Just Business? The Impact of Internet-Specific Strategies on Venture Performance. In *Proceedings of 13th International Conference for the Management of Technology,* April 2004.

33. Grahm, L. and Metaxs, T. (2003). Critical Thinking in the Internet Era. *Communications of the ACM, 46,* 5, May.

34. Southhard, P. and Siau, K. (2004). A Survey of On e-Banking Retail Initiatives. *Communications of the ACM, 47,* 10, October.

35. Bock, G. and Marca, D. (1995). *Designing Groupware.* McGraw-Hill.

7

INTERNET-BASED PROCESS

When each part of a business process can quickly make an e-business connection to a cus-tomer or a supplier, the adaptability of the business' operation is maximized. To achieve this goal, the process must (a) be a set of integrated Web pages, (b) exhibit a consistent look and feel, and (c) point to specific software functions and detailed data elements for efficient running. The implementation must also produce files of live performance data, so the process can be monitored in real time. The patterns involved are:

46. Adaptable e-Business Connection
47. e-Business Connection Architecture
48. e-Business Connection Service Level
49. Highly Modular and Granular Process
50. Process Steps as Interconnected Web Pages
51. Process Wrappers around Applications
52. Hyperlinks with Process Knowledge
53. Process Branding and Transparency
54. Process Monitoring Dashboard

The resulting Adaptable e-Business Connection (46) architecture would conceptually look like the one shown in Figure 7. It is implemented via a Highly Modular and Granular Process (49), in which each process step is a Web page.

HOW TO INTERPRET FRAMEWORK #7

Business adaptability results when a company can, at any time it wishes to, create an Adaptable Business Connection (46) to any other company. This requires, first and fore-most, a predefined e-Business Connection Architecture (47) that explains in detail how two companies electronically connect, plus an e-Business Connection Service Level (48) that spells out how fast and how well that connection must perform. For maximum

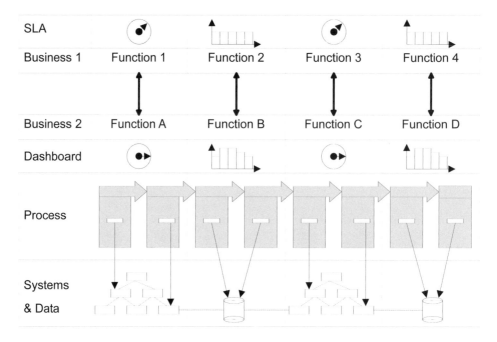

Figure 7. Framework #7: Adaptable e-business connection architecture.

adaptability, the design of the connection should rely on a Highly Modular and Granular Process (49) that is implemented with Process Steps as Interconnected Web Pages (50).

If a company has designed its software applications to be adaptable, Process Wrappers Around Applications (51) are possible, thus enabling the "opening up" of operations to customers, channels, suppliers, and employees. A process wrapper is a process step that is implemented as a distinct Web page. This Web page can contains hyperlinks to other process Web pages as well as a description of detailed procedures. The Web page may also contain hyperlinks to one or more software functions. Each such software function is therefore "wrapped" by the process.

When a process is implemented as Web pages, Hyperlinks with Process Knowledge (52) become visible to customers, channels, suppliers, and employees. Every process keyword and supporting document is made accessible to every process user This technique also permits easy Process Branding and Transparency (53), which is essential when many business-to-business connections are required to respond to a Business Event (55). This occurs when processes further down in the chain assume the visual appearance of their parent process Web page. We call this "inheritance" of visual properties, and it comes about automatically when object-oriented design practices are followed.

Process Web pages also permit the easy implementation of a Process Monitoring Dashboard (54), which means that a company can remotely monitor the operations of its suppliers, suppliers to those suppliers, and so on. Therefore, the design comes full circle—the connection is first defined, its measures are defined, it is implemented with Web pages that can be monitored, and the monitoring data become the measurement.

The remainder of this chapter details each of the patterns that, together, create Framework #7.

Pattern 46. Adaptable e-Business Connection

An e-business connection implements a link in the Value Chain (25).[1] Today, connections are at risk when (a) the business partnership is incorrectly designed, (b) the process is not implemented quickly enough, or (c) the operation cannot adapt to changes in business direction.[2]

> *An adaptable e-business connection must permit an immediate entity-to-entity hookup at any point in the entire business process.*

For example, the connection produces an architecture for the business relationship,[16] and creates processes within the architecture. "Adaptable" means that design constantly mirrors and supports the relationship.

Therefore, Selectively Open and Close (3) your business by creating an Adaptable e-Business Connection (46) to Enable Response to Change and Risk (12) via an Outsourced Process (16). Monitor supplier performance with Derived Performance and Savings Metrics (4).

Pattern 47. e-Business Connection Architecture

Adaptable e-business connections are created by using an architecture that addresses all constraints: intent of the partnership,[3] operational policies,[2] procedural assumptions,[4] data formats,[5] interface standards,[6] and performance metrics.[1] It establishes both boundary and hookup.

> *An e-business connection architecture defines a complete boundary, including entities, policies, and market forces.*

For example, it defines the roles each partner plays and the policies that dictate response time. Customers, suppliers, substitute products, regulatory shifts, and economic cycles can all appear in the architecture.[7] The intent is to define everything that could affect the business partnership.

Therefore, modularize your e-Business Connection Architecture (47). Define all business-to-business connection interfaces, and all factors that can affect each interface point. Know exactly which functions comprise the Outsourced Process (16), and whether you are implementing an Online Business (44) or an Internet Business (45).

Pattern 48. e-Business Connection Service Level

Partnering firms may fail to anticipate conflicts or lack of accountability. If an e-Business Connection (46) lacks a measurable process, outcomes may become counterproductive. This can range from gridlock or stalemate to an unimaginative compromise to which no one is really committed.[8]

> *The e-business connection architecture definition must contain the service level agreement for that connection.*

For example, successful contract labor programs are measured against well-defined metrics (e.g., fill ratio, response time, cost compliance) that apply to all labor suppliers. Thus, the overall performance of the program is simply the sum of the individual supplier performances.

Therefore, define a Master Agreement (18) with direct Flow-Down (20) of Performance Metrics (21). Ensure that the service level is the same for the Outsourced Process (16) owner and for all Supplier Subtiers (24).

Pattern 49. Highly Modular and Granular Process

Once the connection, its architecture, and expected performance have been defined, the e-process is then designed. The e-process is unlike traditional processes—it is both hierarchic and networked, and it is very modular and granular.[8] Later patterns will show how this is achieved.

> *Design a very detailed, hierarchic, and networked process for the*
> *e-business connection. Make each step succinct and measurable.*

For example, lists, phrases, brief sentences, and very short paragraphs are more effective than lengthy narratives.[8] Traditional process modeling methods can produce very detailed hierarchies. Defining process steps as hyperlinked Web pages yields a tightly connected network of steps.

Therefore, create a Highly Modular and Granular Process (49) via a hierarchic process model of the Adaptable e-Business Connection (46) comprising Process Steps as Interconnected Web Pages (50).

Pattern 50. Process Steps as Interconnected Web Pages

Used in tandem, hierarchic process modeling,[4] deep Web structures,[9] and process as hypercode[8] create the e-process. Careful modeling[17] isolates the business rules each process step needs. Hyperlinks[15] create the logical network needed to traverse Web pages[10] during execution.

> *Turn each process step into a web page. Make all business rules explicit.*
> *Hyperlink all pages so the collection can be navigated using just a browser*
> *and be executed by a person or a machine.*

For example, when generated automatically from process models, consistent hyperlinks can be created for process step names, business rule definitions, data objects, and software application GUI screens.

Therefore, use hierarchic process modeling to uncover the essential business rules the e-process needs. Use hyperlinks to create a highly networked set of Web pages designed to be traversed and executed.

Pattern 51. Process Wrappers around Applications

When business process is separated from software, a specific process step can be hyperlinked to a specific application screen.[5] This "opens up" the software, permitting each function (not the whole application) to be accessed right where it is required in the process.[8]

> *Implement Web-based applications that allow each GUI screen to be*
> *potentially referenced by a hyperlink on a process Web page.*

For example, there is no need for a person to navigate a complex application menu tree to get to the software function needed to adjust a time card when that person knows that is what they must do next. Most of the time, people know the function they need; they just need access to it.

Therefore, allow each software function, data object, and e-form to be activated by a hyperlink on a process Web page. This "wraps" the process around software and data, so users first have to know the process rationale before executing software or changing data.

Pattern 52. Hyperlinks with Process Knowledge

Process users are vary in their process knowledge.[11,12] Expert users know it well, intermittent users have incomplete knowledge, and infrequent users must always learn it.[2,5] To accommodate[13] all users, hyperlinks with semantic knowledge[8,18] on Web pages should be color-coded.

> *Use colored hyperlinks to distinguish inputs, outputs, business rules,*
> *software applications, e-forms, data objects, and process steps.*

For example, multicolored links help novice users learn the process. Infrequent users create reminders by making all links the same color. Experts override multiple colors with the hover color, causing descriptions to read as plain text, yet keywords light up when the mouse passes by.

Therefore, encode process semantic knowledge into all hyperlinks by using color. Allow end users to personalize their browsers to use or override the color scheme to aid process learning or remembering.

Pattern 53. Process Branding and Transparency

It is a straightforward engineering matter to separate the content of a business process from its look and feel.[14] This separation is critical because it enables the business to Selectively Open and Close (3) the process dynamically, without additional design or implementation.[8]

> *Always separate process content (e.g., process steps, rules, and links) from*
> *look and feel (e.g., menu location, color scheme, and text layout).*

For example, a "style template" is the current tool for encoding look and feel. When a company's brand is encoded in such a template, the brand can be placed on any Web page, including those of suppliers. In this way, brand transparency across the end-to-end process is achieved.

Therefore, isolate the company's brand design into a "style template," which can be applied to all process Web pages. Apply the brand across the company and across the relevant processes of all suppliers.

Pattern 54. Process Monitoring Dashboard

The e-Business Connection Architecture (47) defines responses. The Highly Modular and Granular Process (49) defines response metrics. Hyperlinks with Process Knowledge (52) point to metric data. Thus, the process monitoring dashboard is created using these three elements.[8]

> *Create a process monitoring dashboard to show how well the process meets the e-business connection service level (48).*

For example, if the files containing Performance Metrics (21) data are dynamically updated while the process is being executed, any link in the Value Chain (25) can be monitored in real time, regardless of the distance between the executing entity and the monitoring entity. The dashboard is the monitoring tool. It provides an appropriate display for the real-time value of each metric.[8]

Therefore, create a Process Monitoring Dashboard (54) using the files containing live Performance Metrics (21), using the ability to record Web page hits, and using cookies to understand end user behavior.

IMPLICATIONS OF PATTERN USE

An Adaptable e-Business Connection (46) should be the design goal for an e-business solution or one of its components. The detailed design for the connection evolves from an e-Business Connection Architecture (47) that explicitly maps those business-to-business functions and rules required to implement the connection.

Each function in the connection has a Highly Modular and Granular Process (49), and each implements Process Steps as Interconnected Web Pages (50). Each function has an e-Business Connection Service Level (48), the sum of which appears on a Process Monitoring Dashboard (54). Each function also has a set of business rules that assist (i.e., help the function complete its operation) and constrain (i.e., ensure the function operates within corporate and industry guidelines).

Process Wrappers Around Applications (51) simplify an implementation, because specific software functions deep inside an application are made available via Hyperlinks with Process Knowledge (52). This design approach makes easy the subsequent task of implementing Process Branding and Transparency (53). This means that software functions operate within a process wrapper, and the company with the primary customer relationship wraps its brand around all functions that operate during the Business Response (56).

REFERENCES

1. Poirier, C. (1999). *Advanced Supply Chain Management.* Publishers Group West.

2. Marca, D. and Perdue, B. (1997). Business-to-Business Connections. *Software Engineering Tech Council Newsletter, 15,* 3, March.

3. Kalakota, R. and Whinston, A. (1996). *Frontiers of Electronic Commerce.* Addison-Wesley.

4. Marca, D. and McGowan, C. (1992). *IDEF0: Business Process and Enterprise Modeling.* Eclectic Solutions, Inc.

5. Marca, D. and Perdue, P. (2000). A Software Engineering Approach and Tool Set for Develop-

ing Internet Applications. In *IEEE 22nd International Conference on Software Engineering,* June 2002.

6. Alencar, P. (2002). A Logical Theory of Interfaces and Objects. *IEEE Transactions on Software Engineering,* June.

7. Jayachandra, Y. (1994). *Re-Engineering the Networked Enterprise.* McGraw-Hill.

8. Marca, D. (2003). Software Engineering Experiences While Implementing Internet-based Business Processes. In *Proceedings of CCT'03,* August 2003.

9. Singh, M. (2002). Deep Web Structure. *IEEE Internet Computing,* September–October.

10. Jourdan, M. (1999). Authoring Techniques for Temporal Scenarios of Multimedia Documents. Handbook of Internet and Multimedia, IEEE Press.

11. Wynblatt, M. (1999). Multimedia Applications on the Internet. In *Handbook of Internet and Multimedia,* IEEE Press.

12. Trigg, R. (1988). Tools for Communicating in a Hypertext Environment. In *Conference on Computer Supported Cooperative Work,* September 1988.

13. Ardissono, L. (2002). Personalization in Business-to-Customer Interaction. *Communications of the ACM,* May.

14. Billus, D. (2002). Adaptive Interfaces for Ubiquitous Web Access. *Communications of the ACM,* May.

15. Schmid, H. and Rossi, G. (2004). Modeling and Designing Processes in e-Commerce Applications. *IEEE Internet Computing,* January–February.

16. Rust, R. and Kannan, P. (2003). E-Service: A New Paradigm for Business in the Electronic Environment. *Communications of the ACM, 46,* 6, June.

17. Agarwal, R., De, P., and Sinha, A. (1999). Comprehending Object and Process Models. *IEEE Transactions on Software Engineering, 25,* 4, July–August.

18. Calado, P., Ribeiro-Neto, B., and Ziviani, N. (2003). Local Versus Global Link Information in the Web. *ACM Transactions on Information Systems, 21,* 1, January.

8

OPEN PROCESS ARCHITECTURE

One crucial factor for the business durability discussed in Chapter 1 is a highly open process architecture. Since today's computing technology is adaptable, an open process architecture is now possible. However, an adaptable process is not automatic; it must be very carefully designed. Fortunately, the design patterns are well known and come from the design of the Internet itself, and prior to that, client/server computing. The patterns are:

55. Business Event
56. Business Response
57. Responses Share the Process
58. Network of Process Web Pages
59. Hyperlinks to Application GUIs
60. Hyperlinks to Web-based Forms
61. Application Logic Separate from GUI
62. Application Logic Separate from Data
63. Transactions Separate from Decisions

The resulting e-process architecture would conceptually look like that in Figure 8. Each Business Response (56), whether manual or automated, is implemented as a Web page, which is hyperlinked to the enterprise-wide Network of Process Web Pages (58). These Web pages, in turn, are hyperlinked to system interfaces—GUI and e-forms for manual response, and application programming interfaces (APIs) for automated response.

HOW TO INTERPRET FRAMEWORK #8

Business adaptability in the 21st century requires an open process architecture that has four distinct tiers.

The first tier, the business tier, is responsible for detecting each and every Business Event (55) and generating an appropriate Business Response (56) for each event.

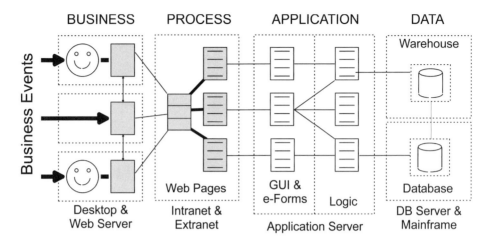

Figure 8. Framework #8: Process Web pages link responses to systems.

The second tier, the process tier, enables each response to share any or all portions of the business process, which is implemented as a Network of Process Web Pages (58).

The third tier, the application tier, houses software logic. Sometimes the interface to this software is through a graphical user interface (GUI), and sometimes it is through an application programming interface (API). Regardless of the interface method, all software is designed to keep Application Logic Separate from GUI (61). Similarly, software is designed to keep Application Logic Separate from Data (62).

The fourth tier, the data tier, distinguishes the data required to complete transactions—all the data required to fully complete a Business Response (56)—from the data required to remember customers and make decisions. From this distinction comes the design principle of keeping Transactions Separate from Decisions (63).

The remainder of this chapter details each of the patterns that, together, create Framework #8.

Pattern 55. Business Event

Computer solutions for business in the 21st century are primarily event–response in nature.[1] In other words, information processing is secondary to the objective of real-time[15] response to business events.[2] Therefore, open process architecture design starts at the events[14] level.

Define all business events, and define how each is measured and reported.

For example, some business events for contract labor management are "need contingent labor," "request contingent labor," "person selected," "assignment started," and "assignment ended." Some metrics are "average requisition fill time" and "assignment duration." When events are not defined, responses become complex, ineffective, or inefficient.

Therefore, create a distinct definition for each Business Event (55). This way, one Business Response (56) can be defined for each event and, thus, Performance and Savings Metrics (4) can be easily defined.

Pattern 56. Business Response

Responding to events is the primary goal[3] of the operational component of a business, and each response must be designed to proactively[4] handle each event. To maximize adaptability, the logic for each response must be modular (i.e., separate from all the others).

> *Define one response for each business event. Document each definition as a Web page. Put all Web pages on people's desktops or on Web servers.*

For example, some business responses for contract labor management are "request contingent labor," "submit candidate," "onboard selected person," and "notify contractor of assignment end."

Therefore, define one Business Response (56) for each Business Event (55). This way, each response definition is kept modular, which greatly simplifies personnel training and process maintenance.

Pattern 57. Responses Share the Process

Although each response has a modular design, the behavior of any particular response might intersect[5] with one or more other responses. In other words, responses might, and usually do, share portions of the entire set of standardized[12] business process activities.[6]

> *For each response, create hyperlinks to those parts of the end-to-end business process that are used to implement the response.*

For example, the process step "validate person's social security number" is a process shared by the responses "onboard selected person" and "notify contractor of assignment end," as well as others.

Therefore, so that Responses Share the Process (57), make sure the end-to-end business process is highly modular. This means carefully decomposing it into a well-organized hierarchy of atomic process steps.

Pattern 58. Network of Process Web Pages

Process adaptability and efficiency[13] are maximized with a Highly Modular and Granular Process (49). This approach creates a tightly integrated network[7] of Web pages. Integration occurs because each process Web page has explicit hyperlinks to other process Web pages.

> *Document the end-to-end business process as a network of interconnected Web pages. Put all Web pages on the Internet.*

For example, first define a Web page for each atomic process step. Then define a Web page for an aggregate of atomic process steps. Then define a Web page for an aggregate of aggregates. This "bottom-up" activity results in a hierarchically structured, Web-based process.

Therefore, create a Network of Process Web Pages (58) by creating a Web page for each atomic process step, and each aggregate, until you have a hierarchical Internet Version of Your Business (2) process.

Pattern 59. Hyperlinks to Application GUIs

Those process steps supported by automation should contain explicit hyperlinks to application user interfaces[8] (i.e., GUIs). These links point directly to the specific screen needed for the process step. There is no need to always require a person to navigate the application's menu.

> *For each process Web page, create hyperlinks to any required application.*
> *Make each hyperlink point to a specific screen inside the software*
> *application.*

For example, each GUI screen of a Web-based application is, in fact, a URL. This means that it is possible for a process step to hyperlink directly to the specific application screen or screens[8] without having to go through the application's functional hierarchy or menu tree.

Therefore, create Hyperlinks to Application GUIs (59) so that the process user is brought directly to the screen needed to accomplish the activity. This "opens up" your business' software application portfolio, turning it into a more Highly Adaptable Technology Platform (6).

Pattern 60. Hyperlinks to Web-based Forms

Sometimes, complex application user interfaces are not required to support a process step and a hyperlink to an electronic form[8] is all that is needed. The e-form acts as the user interface to the data object that a process step requires. Data creation, reading, updating, deleting, and e-mailing are, thus, handled in a straightforward manner.

> *For each process Web page, create hyperlinks to any required Web-based*
> *forms. Put all Web-based forms on a server.*

For example, the essential data objects for contract labor management are often implemented as Web-based forms: "requisition," "candidate submittal," "assignment," "time card," "expense report," and "invoice." Experience with object-oriented solutions for contract labor[8] has shown that end users can naturally think about their data in terms of objects.

Therefore, create Hyperlinks to Web-based Forms (60) whenever a form can do the job instead of an application. Use the Application Logic Separate from Data (62) pattern to isolate each form from its data.

Pattern 61. Application Logic Separate from GUI

Adaptability is increased when the architecture is not embedded in the applications.[9] To accomplish this, application logic is separated from the application GUI. The logic is implemented as highly modular "stored procedures" that are shared across the entire application portfolio.

> *For each application and Web-based form, separate the GUI from the*
> *underlying software application logic. Make the application logic highly*
> *modular.*

For example, most contract labor management solutions separate a form from its workflow logic. Some typical workflows are "requisition approval," "candidate approval," and "time card approval."

Therefore, keep Application Logic Separate from GUI (61) logic. Also, Separate GUI Event Handling from the GUI Logic (78). Implement this pattern as a set of Reusable Procedures Written in XML, Java, or SQL (83) so that all applications and Web-based forms can use the software.

Pattern 62. Application Logic Separate from Data

Application logic also needs separation from the data in order to effectively and efficiently share data across the application portfolio.[10] This is done by having application logic access reusable data objects, whose logic is, in turn, separated from the actual database.

> *For each application logic module, separate its computational logic from the logic that manages transactional data.*

For example, the procedure-oriented logic that uses the Standard Pricing Table (23) to determine the validity of a requisition is a quite distinct from the data-oriented logic required to maintain that table.

Therefore, use Physically Distinct Software Layers (76) to keep Application Logic Separate from Data (62). Implement application logic with Reusable Procedures Written in XML, Java, or SQL (83). Use objects to Modularize the Data Access Logic (80).

Pattern 63. Transactions Separate from Decisions

Those event–response systems that operate extremely fast must rely on transactional databases that are designed to be updated almost instantly. To ensure that the constant stream of updates is unimpeded,[11] the data for reporting are kept in separate databases. This way, decision making (which relies on reporting) never interferes with transactions.

> *Separate software logic that manages transactional data from software logic that manages decision-making data.*

For example, contract labor management solutions generate a lot of transactional data (e.g., requisitions, assignments, timecards) in real time. In addition, Derived Performance and Savings Metrics (4) are highly complex. Therefore, running such reports on the same computers that support the real-time transactions will impact Business Response (56).

Therefore, keep Transactions Separate from Decisions (63). Always Separate Transactional Data from Reporting Data (81), and never let data analysis or reporting activities slow down Business Response (56).

IMPLICATIONS OF PATTERN USE

An Adaptable e-Business Connection (46) requires a defined Business Response (56) for each defined Business Event (55). These Responses Share the Process (57), which is a Network of Process Web Pages (58). The result is a highly adaptable open process architecture.

All process Web pages contain Hyperlinks to Application GUIs (59) or Hyperlinks to Web-based Forms (60). These hyperlinks are placed exactly at the point in the process where an application function or data are needed. This is significant. Currently, people are forced to interact with complex applications to get to the exact function or data they need. The open process architecture eliminates the extra software. It creates a direct connection from the process to a function or data. In addition:

- From a function perspective, care should be taken to keep Application Logic Separate from GUI (61) and to keep Application Logic Separate from Data (62). This maximizes the access and reuse of each function.

- From a data perspective, care should also be taken to keep Transactions Separate from Decisions (63), so that performance does not degrade when complex analysis or reporting must occur while transactions are taking place.

REFERENCES

1. Abrahams, A., Eyers, D., and Bacon, J. (2002). An Asynchronous Rule-based Approach for Business Process Automation Using Obligations. In *Proceedings of the 2002 ACM SIGPLAN Workshop on Rule-based Programming,* October 2002.

2. Cilia, M. and Buchmann, A. (2002). Data Management Issues in Electronic Commerce: Active Functionality Service for e-Business Applications. *ACM SIGMOD Record, 31,* 1, March.

3. Jacobs, S. and Holten R. (1985). Goal Driven Business Modeling: Supporting Decision Making Within Information Systems Development. In *Proceedings of the Conference on Organizational Computing Systems,* August 1995.

4. Adii, A., Botzer, D., Etzion, O., and Yatzkar-Haham, T. (2001). Monitoring Business Processes Through Event Correlation Based on Dependency Model. In *Proceedings of the 2001 ACM SIGMOD Conference on Data Management,* Vol. 30, No. 2, May 2001.

5. Lee, E. and Sangiovanni-Vincentelli, A. (1996). Comparing Models of Computation. In *Proceedings of the 1996 IEEE/ACM International Conference on Computer-Aided Design,* May 1996.

6. Morrison, J., Pirolli, P., and Card, S. (2001). A Taxonomic Analysis of What World Wide Web Activities Significantly Impact People's Decisions and Actions. In *CHI '01 Extended Abstracts on Human factors in Computing Systems,* March 2001.

7. Stefanov, T. and Deprettere, E. (2003). Deriving Process Networks from Weakly Dynamic Applications. In *Proceedings of the 11th International Conference on Hardware/Software Co-design & System Synthesis,* October 2003.

8. Marca, D. (2003). Software Engineering Experiences While Implementing Internet-based Business Processes. In *Proceedings of CCT'03,* August 2003.

9. Stefanov, T., Kienhuis, B., and Deprettere, E. (2002). Advances in System Specification and System Design Frameworks. In *Proceedings of the 10th International Conference on Hardware/Software Co-design & System Synthesis,* October 2003.

10. Gawlick, D. and Shailendra Mishra, S. (2003). Database Issues for Event-based Middleware. In *Proceedings of the 2nd International Workshop on Distributed Event-based Systems,* June 2003.

11. Adelberg, B., Garcia-Molina, H., and Kao, B. (1995). Applying Update Streams in a Soft Real-Time Database System. In *Proceedings of the 1995 ACM SIGMOD International Conference on Management of Data,* Vol. 24, No. 2, May 1995.

12. Patil, S. and Newcomer, E. (2003). ebXML and Web Services. *IEEE Internet Computing, 7,* 3, May–June.

13. Krovi, R., Chandra, A., and Rajagopalan, B. (2003). Information Flow Parameters for Managing Organizational Processes. *Communications of the ACM, 46,* 2, February.

14. Cleland-Hang, J., Chang, C., and Christensen, M. (2003). Event-Based Traceability for Managing Evolutionary Change. *IEEE Transactions on Software Engineering, 29,* 9, September.

15. Tsang, M., Fitzmaurice, G., Kurtenbach, G., and Khan, A. (2003). Game-Like Navigation and Responsiveness in Non-Game Applications. *Communications of the ACM, 46,* 7, July.

III

e-COMMERCE

To accomplish e-Commerce (completing business transactions over open networks), implement a highly adaptable technology platform:

- Create a business architecture (Chapter 9) using autonomous business functions that cooperate via messages to respond to events. Ensure that each maintains its own set of response rules.
- Create a process architecture (Chapter 10) that respond to events via cascading, measurable event–response pairs, implemented as messages between the autonomous business functions.
- Create an open, adaptable software architecture (Chapter 11) by separating GUI, data, and application; modularizing business rules and data objects; and coding all software in XML, Java, or SQL.
- Create a data architecture (Chapter 12) by separating transactional and reporting data, and running reports against a data warehouse.

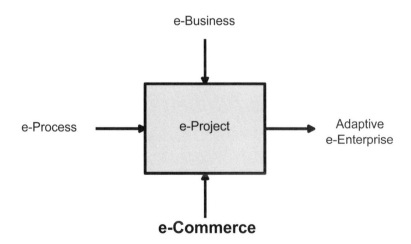

9

BUSINESS ARCHITECTURE

Business architecture is now being recognized for its crucial role in addressing shrinking product life cycles, increasing competition, and individualizing customer needs.[1] A firm must be highly adaptive, especially an e-business. The term "turn on a dime" has been used many times to describe this ability, yet few can articulate what actually must be implemented to achieve high adaptability. At the business level, the key to operational adaptability is creating an organization that simultaneously permits autonomy, cooperation, and control[2] among its business functions. The key to durability is to also maintain a very high degree of control over the evolution[17] of all business functions. The patterns used to achieve this are:

64. Autonomous Business Functions
65. Cooperation via Event–Response Pairs
66. Control via Wholly Owned Business Rules
67. Control via Company-Wide Business Rules
68. Organizational Learning via Rule Revision

The resulting business architecture would conceptually look like the one shown in Figure 9. Notice that the Autonomous Business Functions (64) are discrete entities that operate independently and are controlled by their own business rules as well as by enterprise-wide business rules. The most important characteristic of this business architecture is that the autonomous business functions cooperate by sharing messages on the network. They are not permitted to look at the business rules owned by other autonomous business functions, nor are they allowed to look inside the transactional databases of other functions.

HOW TO INTERPRET FRAMEWORK #9

The rapid creation of an Adaptable Business Connection (46) requires a pre-defined business architecture.

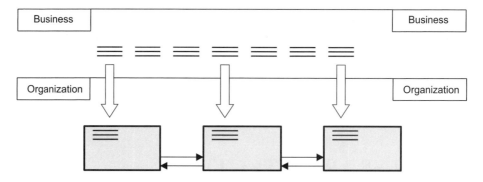

Figure 9. Framework #9: Business functions are autonomous and rule driven.

To maximize adaptability, the business architecture must allow only Autonomous Business Functions (64). This means that any entity of a company, no matter how large or small, is potentially its own function that must cooperate with other functions in order to respond to Business Events (55). Thus, Cooperation via Event–Response Pairs (65) is the mechanism by which a Business Response (56) is ultimately achieved.

Since functions are autonomous, each is controlled by its business rules. Two design principles apply. First, control via wholly owned Business Rules (66) makes each function responsible for understanding what it has to do during each particular Business Response (56). Second, control via company-wide Business Rules (67) makes each function responsible for understanding what standards it must follow during each particular Business Response (56). Therefore, as the autonomous functions, and the company as a whole, gain experience in responding to events, Organizational Learning via Rule Revision (68) also happens.

The remainder of this chapter details each of the patterns that, together, create Framework #9.

Pattern 64. Autonomous Business Functions

Business architecture design starts with the reorganization of a hierarchically structured[11] company into a web of closely interacting functional islands.[3] These autonomous business functions[14] are self-directed work groups[4] integrated by information and material flow.

> *Create as many business functions as you need to respond to all the anticipated events. Ensure that each is an autonomous entity.*

For example, contract labor management has many such functions: fulfillment, assignment management, and time management. Inside each is a collection of more granular functions that participate in one or more responses (e.g., time card adjustment inside time management).

Therefore, create a small, highly modular Autonomous Business Function (64) for each business response. Do not combine functions in an attempt to gain efficiencies, as this will limit the overall adaptability.

Pattern 65. Cooperation via Event–Response Pairs

Autonomous Business Functions (64) become a virtual organization when connected together by a computer network. They cooperate to respond to business events by communicating[5] on that network. Each communication can thus be thought of as an event–response pair.[15,16]

> *Each business function cooperates with other functions via event–response pairs. No other kind of communication is permitted.*

For example, the event–response pair between requisition management and fulfillment is "approved requisition" and "hired candidate." Here, an approved requisition triggers many functions to perform their roles until a suitable person is found, interviewed, and hired—a cascading effect.

Therefore, define explicit event–response pairs as <u>the</u> means by which two autonomous business functions cooperate. Never allow a business function to "look inside" another function for rules or procedures.

Pattern 66. Control via Wholly Owned Business Rules

You can think of each Autonomous Business Function (64) as being an intelligent agent[6] that can be called upon to do its part in responding to a business event. Each function must, therefore, have its own dedicated response knowledge,[7] its rules,[12] which it must constantly maintain.

> *Each business function wholly owns the business rules it alone needs to respond to the events for which it is responsible.*

For example, the requisition distribution function uses its own knowledge about Skill Niches (22) to correctly distribute an approved requisition to only those Supplier Subtiers (24) who have the potential to submit suitable candidates. This is an example of a business rule that needs to be known only at the lowest level of function in the solution.

Therefore, allow each Autonomous Business Function (64) to control itself using its own knowledge about how to respond to events. Require it to perform its own Organizational Learning via Rule Revision (68).

Pattern 67. Control via Company-Wide Business Rules

In addition to its local response knowledge base, an Autonomous Business Function (64) is required to also employ enterprise-wide business rules and industry rules[8] that guide and constrain how all functions must operate during a response to a business event.

> *Each business function uses, without alteration, all the common rules it needs when responding to events for which it is responsible.*

For example, contract labor management solutions include program-wide rules like Performance Metrics (21). One such rule defines the maximum time a customer waits to have a suitable person arrive on the work site after requisition approval. Many autonomous functions affect this metric.

Therefore, require each Autonomous Business Function (64) to also use the Common Body of Knowledge (13). Require the company to perform its own Organizational Learning via Rule Revision (68).

Pattern 68. Organizational Learning via Rule Revision

Organizations are not static. They get reengineered[9] and they also learn.[10] But organizational learning requires direct experience.[10] This can happen only when each Autonomous Business Function (64) revises its response knowledge due what it learns during a response.

> ***When learning occurs after a response to an event, update all relevant wholly owned rules and all company-wide common rules.***

For example, assume that the "time adjustment" function changes a time card after the weekly payroll file has been sent for processing, but it does not know that doing so would result in an incorrect paycheck. Once this is discovered, the function must update its knowledge base.

Therefore, require the company and each Autonomous Business Function (64) to perform its own Organizational Learning via Rule Revision (68) based on the direct experience gained during responses.

IMPLICATIONS OF PATTERN USE

An Adaptable e-Business Connection (46) requires a very flexible and highly adjustable business architecture, comprising sets of Autonomous Business Functions (64), one set of functions for each Business Response (56) to a specific Business Event (55). All the autonomous business functions are expected to:

- Conduct Cooperation Via Event–Response Pairs (65). Functions are not allowed to acquire operational data or business rules that they do not directly own.
- Implement their Control Via Wholly Owned Business Rules (66), or implement Control Via Company-Wide Business Rules (67). Functions are not permitted to see the rules or logic for any other function.
- Implement Organizational Learning Via Rule Revision (68), but only for those business rules that they directly own. Functions are required to keep themselves fully knowledgeable on how to respond to a future Business Event (55) based on how it performed during the last Business Response (56) to that business event.

REFERENCES

1. Kirchner, S. and März, L. (2002). Towards Self-Adaptive Production Systems. *International Journal of Production Research, 40,* 15, October.
2. Keidel, R. (1995). *Seeing Organizational Patterns.* Berrett-Koehler.
3. Peters, P., Szczurko, P., Jarke, M., and Jeusfeld, M. (1995). Business Process Oriented Infor-

mation Management: Conceptual Models at Work. in *Proceedings of Conference on Organizational Computing Systems,* August 1995.

4. Lipnack, J. and Stamps, J. (1994). *The Age of the Network.* Oliver Wight Publications.

5. Ahlsén, M. and Rosengren, P. (1995). The Architecture of Worknets. *ACM SIGOIS Bulletin, 16,* 1, August.

6. Yiming, Y., Prabir, N., Jun-Jang, J., and Santhosh, K. (2003). Smart Distance Principle for "Sense and Respond" Enterprise Systems. *Web Intelligence & Agent Systems, 1,* 2, June.

7. Griggs, K. and Wild, R. (2003). Intelligent Support for Sophisticated e-Commerce Services. *e-Service Journal, Vol. 2,* 2, December.

8. Arsanjani, A. and Ng, D. (2002). Business Compilers: Towards Supporting a Highly Reconfigurable Service-Oriented Architecture. In *Proceedings of the 17th Annual ACM SIGPLAN Conference on Object-Oriented Programming,* November 2002.

9. Hammer, M. and Champy, J. (1993). *Reengineering the Corporation.* Harper Collins nc.

10. Senge, P. (1990). *The Fifth Discipline: The Art and Practice of the Learning Organization.* Doubleday Currency Publishing.

11. Batory, D., Sarvela, J., and Rauschmayer. (2004). Scaling Step-Wise Refinement. *IEEE Transactions on Software Engineering, 30,* 6, June.

12. Drislane, D. (2004). Business Rules: Leveraging Your Pervasive Operational Asset. In *Proceedings of 13th International Conference for the Management of Technology,* April 2004.

13. Cetindamar, D. (2004). Learning Through E: Organizational Learning in Implementation. In *Proceedings of 13th International Conference for the Management of Technology,* April 2004.

14. McCrickard, D., Chewar, C., Somervell, J., and Ndiwalana, A. (2003). A Model for Notification Systems Evaluation—Assessing User Goals for Multitasking Activity. *ACM Transactions on Human-Computer Interaction, 10,* 4, December.

15. Cleland-Hang, J., Chang, C., and Christensen, M. (2003). Event-Based Traceability for Managing Evolutionary Change. *IEEE Transactions on Software Engineering, 29,* 9, September.

16. Tsang, M., Fitzmaurice, G., Kurtenbach, G., and Khan, A. (2003). Game-Like Navigation and Responsiveness in Non-Game Applications. *Communications of the ACM, 46,* 7, July.

17. Anton, A. and Price, R. (2003). Functional Paleontology: The Evolution of User-Visible System Services. *IEEE Transactions on Software Engineering, 29,* 2, February.

10

PROCESS ARCHITECTURE

The number of variables that affect the corporate bottom line appears to be growing at an exponential rate1, and one of those variables is adaptable processes. Adaptable and efficient processes[17] are essential for e-commerce, because they enable a company to respond to its business events whenever and wherever they occur. Such processes are a networks[2,3] of autonomous functions that can dynamically connect themselves together via messages whenever a business event occurs. The patterns involved are:

69. Anywhere, Anytime Business Events
70. Respond at Point and Time of Event
71. Measurable Event–Response Pairs
72. Messages Implement Event–Response Pairs
73. Only Pass Messages to Respond to Events
74. Comprehensive Web Site for Each Function
75. All Needed Operating Rules on Each Web Site

The resulting process architecture would conceptually look like that in Figure 10. Notice how a Business Event (55) activates an autonomous function, which in turn triggers one or more other Autonomous Business Functions (64). The architecture the figure has been simplified. In a real company, there are hundreds of autonomous business functions. Each function knows all the responses in which it participates. Each function also knows which autonomous business functions it must trigger to help it complete its part on each specific Business Response (56). All triggers are implemented as Measurable Event–Response Pairs (71).

HOW TO INTERPRET FRAMEWORK #10

The rapid creation of an Adaptable Business Connection (46) requires a predefined, highly modularized process architecture. To maximize adaptability, the process architecture must be able to detect Business Dvents (55) anywhere and any time they occur, and it must also strive to Respond at the Point and Time of Event (70). This means that Perfor-

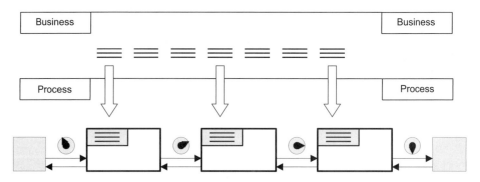

Figure 10. Framework #10: Autonomous functions respond to business events.

mance Metrics (21) can be defined for each event–response pair of autonomous functions. To enable this measurement, Messages Implement Event–Response Pairs (72) and functions are required to Only Pass Messages to Respond to Events (73). The process used by autonomous functions to respond to a Business Event (55) is housed in a Comprehensive Web Site for Each Function (74). Taken together, all of these design principles create a highly modularized process architecture. Since it is highly modular, the business process can be replicated and distributed across the entire enterprise as needed to maximize response.

The remainder of this chapter details each of the patterns that, together, create Framework #10.

Pattern 69. Anywhere, Anytime Business Events

Business events[15] now extend across an enterprise[4] and across space and time.[5] The resulting response network must, therefore, be complete, secure, flexible, scalable, and interoperable.[6] It must even reconfigure itself to follow events from location to location and context to context.[7]

> *Consider the geography and time frame for each business event. Whenever possible, do not restrict their scope.*

For example, when a time card is implemented as an e-form, the event "time entry" can occur anywhere and anytime a contractor can access a networked computer. Imagine how important this is for Canada's largest energy company, which has contractors in the remote corners of the Artic. With Internet technology "7 by 24" and worldwide operations are possible.

Therefore, analyze each Business Event (55) for its geographic and temporal properties. Design a specific Business Response (56) to address all of these properties. Keep the design as general as possible.

Pattern 70. Respond at Point and Time of Event

Adaptable end-to-end e-commerce processes are able to respond almost instantly[20] to a business event at the exact place and time of its occurrence.[8] Their design lets them address user context and disconnection,[15] and their ability to be ready to immediately re-spond makes them cost-effective.

> ***Attempt to respond as close as possible to the point at which the event occurred. Avoid delays due to distance and time.***

For example, Progressive Insurance Company put its automobile claim agents in cars with networked computers. When notified of an accident, they drive to that location or to where the person was going. Typically within 15 minutes, the agent settles the claim and a check is in the person's hand! The resulting drop in fixed assets (i.e., buildings) lowered operating costs.

Therefore, design each Business Response (56) to occur as close as possible to its Business Event (55). Ensure Control Via Wholly Owned Business Rules (66) and Com-pany-Wide Business Rules (67).

Pattern 71. Measurable Event–Response Pairs

To achieve durability, a company must measure itself to improve. This is doubly true for the e-commerce process. It must be monitored[9,15] everywhere it responds to a business event, and everywhere it permits access to real-time data for making transactions and de-cisions.[10]

> ***Define metrics for each event–response pair. Whenever possible, reuse existing metrics. Avoid creating esoteric metrics.***

For example, contract labor fulfillment comprises many functions (e.g., distribute req-uisition, submit candidate, interview person, select person, hire person, bring the person onboard). With computers, the duration of each function can be tracked to the second, which would be impossible if done manually. This capability gives the human resources department a tool to enforce their policies.

Therefore, define a metric for each event–response pair. Whenever possible, reuse metrics, especially the Derived Performance and Savings Metrics (4) and any existing supplier Performance Metrics (21).

Pattern 72. Messages Implement Event–Response Pairs

Measuring events[9] and their responses is not possible without some kind of formalism.[10] Computer technology formalizes connections using messages[19] that are sent between peo-ple and/or software system functions. Each message should be defined to formalize just one event and its corresponding response.

> ***Implement event–response pairs using message technology. Define messages to be clear, concise, and unambiguous.***

For example, time card approval comprises many functions (e.g., time entry, approve time, reject time, resubmit time card). At each step, the time card object is passed from one person's computer to the other via messages that also pass the workflow status of the timecard.

Therefore, an Appropriate Use of Middleware and SQL (77) will best implement an event–response pair as one or more messages. Strictly adhere to standards to ensure Measurable Event–Response Pairs (71).

Pattern 73. Only Pass Messages to Respond to Events

Although only some business functions are designated to receive an event, the whole process (i.e., the peer-to-peer network of functions[11]) is ready to aid in the response. When help is needed, a function sends a message to another function,[14,16] which may send a message, and so on.

> *When autonomous functions need help to respond to a business event, pass messages to other functions. Never look inside another function (i.e., its rules and its transactional data) in order to respond.*

For example, an online order entry function can simultaneously ask the billing function if the customer has paid prior invoices on time, and the inventory function if enough product is on hand. The order entry process trusts each function to look at its own data and send an answer via a message. This kind of design, though not commonly practiced today, yields the most modular of solutions. Each operational component of the solution becomes a functional object, having the same properties we associate with data objects: modularity, autonomy, brevity, and reliability.

Therefore, rely on Instantaneous Networks (37) to transmit messages among Autonomous Business Functions (64) to complete a Business Response (56). Never use a function's internal rules or transactional data in an attempt to optimize the process.

Pattern 74. Comprehensive Web Site for Each Function

A business cannot respond to its events without process knowledge.[5] Thus, it is crucial for each business function to have its own Web site, which stores the process knowledge (coded in XML[18] or Java) and has appropriate interfaces for use by people and/or systems.

> *Implement a Web site for each business function to enable it to respond to all events for which it is responsible.*

For example, the function that screens a time card looks at daily hours worked to see if they conform to state law. When the rules are coded in Java with a user interface that lets people easily read the rules, this allows either manual or automated screening, whichever is called for. This design maximizes a business' options for connecting to other firms.

Therefore, include operating rules, written in XML or Java, in the Web site for the Autonomous Business Function (64). Ensure that these rules invoke the Reusable Procedures Written in XML, Java, or SQL (83).

Pattern 75. All Needed Operating Rules on Each Web Site

Companies have difficulty managing the close yet flexible connections required to conduct e-commerce,[12] and customized connections are expensive and inflexible.[13] These problems are solved when a function has all its own rules, and all company-wide rules, on its own Web site.

> ***Place all required business rules on a business function's Web site.***
> ***Include all common business rules, as appropriate.***

For example, a firm defines the labor type (e.g., exempt, nonexempt) for each job, a contract labor program defines when weekly payroll is sent, and state law defines overtime rules. The time card screening function needs these rules to operate correctly. Rules are the operational "glue."

Therefore, include the Common Body of Knowledge (13) in the Web site for the Autonomous Business Function (64). Ensure that these rules invoke the Reusable Procedures Written in XML, Java, or SQL (83).

IMPLICATIONS OF PATTERN USE

An Adaptable e-Business Connection (46) requires an adaptable process architecture, designed to handle Anywhere, Anytime Business Events (69) via processes that Respond at Point and Time of Event (70). The resulting architecture is, thus, a carefully organized collection of highly specialized event–response pairs that can span the globe, and can detect and respond to events in any country and in any time zone.

An adaptable process architecture supports Autonomous Business Functions (64) by ensuring that they Only Pass Messages to Respond to Events (73), by defining Measurable Event–Response Pairs (71) and by guaranteeing that Messages Implement Event–Response Pairs (72).

An adaptable process architecture also supports Autonomous Business Functions (64) by implementing a Comprehensive Web Site for Each Function (74), and by implementing All Needed Operating Rules on Each Web Site (75). These rules are usually in the background, but because they are implemented with Internet technology, they can be brought to the foreground at any time (e.g., for special decision making).

REFERENCES

1. Hatcher, M. (2003). New Corporate Agendas. *Journal of Public Affairs, 3,* 2, February.
2. Jin, Y., Esser, R., and Lakos, C. (2003). Lightweight Consistency Analysis of Dataflow Process Networks. In *Proceedings of the 26th Australasian Computer Science Conference,* Vol. 16, February 2003.
3. Stark, E. (1987). Concurrent Transition System Semantics of Process Networks. In *Proceedings of the 14th ACM SIGPLAN Symposium on Principles of Programming Languages,* October 1987.
4. Aversano, L. and Canfora, G. (2002). Introducing e-Services in Business Process Models. In *Proceedings of the 14th International Conference on Software Engineering and Knowledge Engineering,* July 2002.
5. Rastogi, P. (2002). Knowledge Management and Intellectual Capital as a Paradigm of Value Creation. *Human Systems Management, 21,* 4, April.

6. Siau, K. and Tian, Y. (2004).Supply Chains Integration: Architecture and Enabling Technologies. *Journal of Computer Information Systems, 44,* 3, Spring.

7. Roussos, G., Peterson, D., and Patel, U. (2003). Mobile Identity Management: An Enacted View. *International Journal of Electronic Commerce, 8,* 1, Fall.

8. Sairamesh, J., Goh, S., Stanoi, I., Li, C., and Padmanabhan S. (2002). Commerce and Businesses: Self-Managing, Disconnected Processes and Mechanisms for Mobile e-Business. In *Proceedings of the 2nd International Workshop on Mobile Commerce,* September 2002.

9. Adii, A., Botzer, D., Etzion, O., and Yatzkar-Haham, T. (2001). Monitoring Business Processes Through Event Correlation Based on Dependency Model. In *Proceedings of the 2001 ACM SIGMOD Conference on Data Management,* Vol. 30, No. 2, May 2001.

10. Dewire, D. and Wyzalek, J. (2004). From the Editor. *Information Systems Management, 21,* 2, Spring.

11. Smith, H., Clippinger, J., and Konsynski, B. (2003). Discovering the Value of P2P Technologies. *Communications of AIS, 2003,* 11, June.

12. Hagel, J. (2002). Leveraged Growth: Expanding Sales Without Sacrificing Profits. *Harvard Business Review, 80,* 10, October.

13. Brown, J. and Hagel, J. (2003). Flexible IT, Better strategy. *McKinsey Quarterly,* 4, April.

14. Bolloju, N. (2004). Improving the Quality of Business Object Models Using Collaboration Patterns. *Communications of the ACM, 47,* 7, July.

15. Cleland-Hang, J., Chang, C., and Christensen, M. (2003). Event-Based Traceability for Managing Evolutionary Change. *IEEE Transactions on Software Engineering, 29,* 9, September.

16. Vinoski, S. (2003). Invocation Styles. *IEEE Internet Computing, 7,* 4, July–August.

17. Agarwal, R., De, P., and Sinha, A. (1999). Comprehending Object and Process Models. *IEEE Transactions on Software Engineering, 25,* 4, July–August.

18. Singh, M. (2004). *The Practical Handbook of Internet Computing.* Chapman & Hall Publishers/CRC Press.

19. Vinoski, S. (2004). Is Your Middleware Dead? *IEEE Internet Computing, 8,* 5, September-October.

20. Lowy, A. and Hood, P. (2004). Moving Beyond the Dilemmas of Contingent Work. *Contingent Workforce Strategies, 1,* 4, June.

11

SOFTWARE ARCHITECTURE

Software applications must be able to immediately react to changes in the e-business or the e-process, so they must be designed (prior to their construction[41]) to be adaptable. Research suggests factoring ISO and object-oriented standards[42] into software architectures in order to increase their adaptability.[1] In addition to these standards, the following patterns, whose origins come from adaptable client/server technology,[2] are suggested:

76. Physically Distinct Software Layers
77. Appropriate Use of Middleware and SQL
78. Separate GUI Event Handling from the GUI Logic
79. Separate Application Logic from Business Rules
80. Use Objects to Modularize the Data Access Logic
81. Separate Transactional Data from Reporting Data
82. All Reports Run Against the Data Warehouse
83. Reusable Procedures Written in XML, Java, or SQL

The resulting software architecture would conceptually look like the one in Figure 11. This is a four-tier conceptual architecture mapped to a three-tier physical architecture (i.e., the two database tiers reside on one machine).

HOW TO INTERPRET FRAMEWORK #11

The rapid creation of an Adaptable Business Connection (46) requires a software architecture that "opens up" software applications, making their inner workings directly accessible by Web-based processes. An open application has three distinct physical tiers, each of which is connected to another tier via an appropriate middleware mechanism.[48]

The first physical tier, the graphical user interface (GUI) tier, houses all the GUI logic. However, it also makes a distinction between the software logic that responds to GUI events (e.g., a mouse click) and the software logic that is application specific (e.g., the

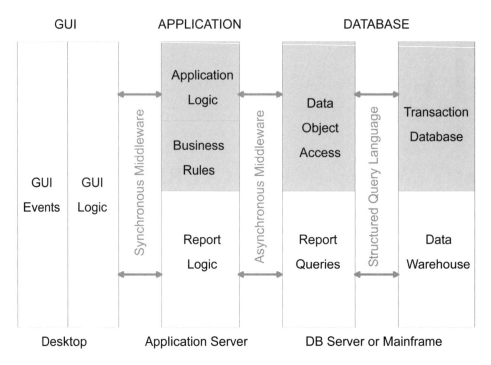

Figure 11. Framework #11: Distinct software tiers communicate via messages.

contents of a skill set pull-down menu changes after the user selects "administrative" or "engineering").

The second physical tier is the application tier. It houses application logic, business rules, and reporting logic. It also keeps separate these three kinds of software. Application logic defines the raw software functions. Business rules define which software functions are executed in what sequence in the context of specific business conditions. Report logic defines how decision-making data must be displayed to end users.

The third physical tier, the database tier, has two logical subtiers. The first logical subtier is the data access subtier, which defines the business data objects and the functions (i.e., methods) that manipulate those objects. It also defines the queries (i.e., software code for business questions) that are used to generate reports. The second logical subtier houses the actual databases. One database is optimized for transaction processing and one is optimized for report generation.

Tying these three layers together are three different types of messaging mechanisms. A message is data that is passed between two software functions according to some protocol. Synchronous messages (the first one completes before the second one starts) go between layer one and layer two, because people operate the GUI in a sequential manner (i.e., they complete one step before doing the next). Asynchronous messages are passed between layer two and layer three to allow software functions to execute without being constrained by the time it takes to access data objects. Structured query language (SQL) is used inside layer three to connect data objects with databases.

The remainder of this chapter details each of the patterns that, together, create Framework #11.

Pattern 76. Physically Distinct Software Layers

An adaptable software architecture has a particular structure, unlike any other. Like all designs, though, it is constrained at various points.[3] The primary constraint creates three distinct sections (called "tiers"): graphical user interface (GUI), application, and database.

> *Create three distinct layers to separate software design and implementation concerns: GUI, applications, and databases.*

For example, a contract labor time card should be implemented as an e-form. This form should invoke application software functions such as verifying the correct hour entry according to state law. The e-form should also be the GUI to a time card object, defining how it is created and changed. Such a design maximizes the modularity of the overall solution in such a way that it also minimizes the effort required to makes future changes.

Therefore, keep Application Logic Separate from GUI (61) and keep Application Logic Separate from Data (62). Consider the Appropriate Use of Middleware and SQL (77) to efficiently connect the three layers.

Pattern 77. Appropriate Use of Middleware and SQL

Distinct tiers require a means of communication. Synchronous[4] (i.e., invoke then wait) middleware[21,29] connects the GUI to the application. Asynchronous[5] (i.e., invoke many functions in parallel) middleware connects the application to data objects. Inside the data tier, structured query language[6,23,24] (SQL) connects data objects to databases.

> *Tie the three software layers together using synchronous middleware, asynchronous middleware, and SQL.*

For example, a GUI event that invokes a procedure must wait for that procedure to finish, but a procedure that invokes a data object should not wait for that data if it can do other useful computations in the interim. Proper messaging can maximize automation while preserving usability.

Therefore, consider the Appropriate Use of Middleware and SQL (77) to efficiently connect the Physically Distinct Software Layers (77) so that Messages Implement Event–Response Pairs (71).

Pattern 78. Separate GUI Event Handling from the GUI Logic

To achieve adaptability and usability,[20,22,37,38,44,46] GUI architectures must be as important as those of the other tiers.[7,43] In particular, the logic that handles button clicks or keystrokes (i.e., GUI event handling) is generic (i.e., it is the same across applications).[8,45] In contrast, the logic used to display esoteric data based on prior user input is application specific.[9,47]

> *Separate GUI event handling (buttons and fields on e-forms) from application-specific GUI logic (Java applets).*

For example, during the typing of a charge number into a time card, there should be no time delay between the keystroke and the visible numbers. But upon completion, a small delay is permissible while the computer performs logic to validate that charge number. The logic used to process GUI events must respond instantly, whereas the logic used to process data entered must ensure a response within conversational limits (i.e., 2 seconds).

Therefore, separate generic, instantaneous response logic of the GUI from that GUI logic which is application specific. Never combine them.

Pattern 79. Separate Application Logic from Business Rules

The principles of modular manufacturing,[10] which advocate modular products, apply to software applications. Specifically, the company-wide business rules that are generic across all applications[2,11] must be modularized so they can be easily shared and centrally maintained.[40]

> *Separate the application-specific logic from business rules. Write all business rules as reusable, stored procedures.*

For example, which suppliers must receive a requisition for a particular labor skill is a business rule. This rule, often a table mapping suppliers to skills, should be a distinct data object to enable multiple procedures to invoke it (e.g., requisition creation, requisition distribution, reporting). The design technique of coding business rules as objects maximizes reuse.

Therefore, encode each element in the Common Body of Knowledge (13) as a distinct procedure that implements that particular business rule. Create Reusable Procedures Written in XML, Java, or SQL (83).

Pattern 80. Use Objects to Modularize the Data Access Logic

Adaptable software applications have no embedded data manipulation logic.[12] Instead, each data object invoked by an application contains its own data manipulation rules[13] (i.e., create, read, update, and delete[2]). The collection of all data objects comprises the data access tier.[39]

> *Isolate data access logic. Modularize it into objects. Define create, read, update, and delete functions for each object.*

For example, the create function for a time card object allows a contractor to create one unique time card for a particular week. Its delete function never allows deletion of the time card object because the time record must be kept for audit purposes. Separating create, read, update, and delete functions isolates the scenarios under which data is transformed.

Therefore, use object-oriented technology to create sharable data objects that modularize their data elements and data manipulation logic. Create Reusable Procedures Written in XML, Java, or SQL (83).

Pattern 81. Separate Transactional Data from Reporting Data

An event–response solution has a data component whose sole concern is extremely fast real-time data updates.[14] That component is optimized for completing transactions immediately. In stark contrast, reporting can involve complex queries[30,36] and intermediate data manipulations.[15,31]

> ***Separate the transactional databases (i.e., updates) from the Data Warehouse (i.e., analyses and reports).***

For example, when a business requires the e-enterprise to fully execute thousands of transactions per second, any reporting done against the transactional database would slow the software down to the point where the business could not operate. It is vital to design this separation at the very onset of the effort. The cost to do this later on is enormous.

Therefore, keep Transactions Separate from Decisions (63). Isolate the Data Warehouse from Transactional Databases (86). Separate the logic that updates the real-time transaction stream from the reporting logic.

Pattern 82. All Reports Run Against the Data Warehouse

A database that is created strictly for reporting purposes is called a data warehouse.[16] It is a restructuring of the transactional data[24,26] into the answers to the business questions being asked by the reports.[17]

> ***Run reports only against the data warehouse. Thoroughly test all report queries to eliminate any errors and inefficiencies, and then reuse them.***

For example, the data warehouse restructures transactional data into dimensions (e.g., product, customer, order, shipment), and also creates new dimensions (e.g., time, geography) to enable "slicing" the data in order to compute metrics or to help people discover trends.

Therefore, implement Derived Performance and Savings Metrics (4) and supplier Performance Metrics (21) as data warehouse reports. Create Reusable Procedures Written in XML, Java, or SQL (83).

Pattern 83. Reusable Procedures Written in XML, Java, or SQL

All components previously mentioned in this chapter are, or contain, procedures. Writing them in XML,[25,26,27,28,32] Java,[33,34,35,42] or SQL[23,24] will maximize their utility (i.e., invoked by the e-process or by applications) and interoperability (i.e., executed by people or machines), and will enable the sharing of process rules across the application portfolio.

> ***Design all software to be reusable. Write all software logic in XML, Java, or SQL. At a minimum, reuse rules, data objects, and queries.***

For example, a procedure written in XML or Java can be viewed in a browser. Thus, it can be a URL, which means it can be invoked by an e-process. This is the way to open up your applications so specific functions, not whole applications, can be invoked by the e-process.

Therefore, create Reusable Procedures Written in XML, Java, or SQL (83) to enable interoperability, process Hyperlinks to Application GUIs (59), and Hyperlinks to Web-based Forms (60).

IMPLICATIONS FOR PATTERN USE

An Adaptable e-Business Connection (46) requires an adaptable software architecture. This architecture is designed as a set of Physically Distinct Software Layers (76), all of which are tied together through the Appropriate Use of Middleware and SQL (77). Additionally, it is the middleware that enables the rapid distribution of solution components across the required business geography. The middleware also enables that distribution to change as soon as the business changes.

The aforementioned software layers are carefully designed to Separate GUI Event Handling from the GUI Logic (78), to Separate Application Logic from Business Rules (79), and to Separate Transactional Data from Reporting Data (81). Furthermore, each software application is designed to Use Objects to Modularize the Data Access Logic (80), and should be implemented via Reusable Procedures Written in XML, Java, or SQL (83). Finally, the software is designed so that All Reports Run Against the Data Warehouse (82), not the transactional databases.

REFERENCES

1. Losavio, F., Chirinos, L., Matteo, A., Lévy, N., and Ramdane-Cherif, A. (2004). Designing Quality Architecture: Incorporating ISO Standards into the Unified Process. *Information Systems Management, 21,* 1, Winter.
2. Gold-Bernstein, B. and Marca, D. *Designing Client/Server Systems.* Prentice-Hall.
3. Stefanov, T., Kienhuis, B., and Deprettere, E. (2002). Advances in System Specification and System Design Frameworks. In *Proceedings of the 10th International Symposium on Hardware/Software Co-design,* May 2002.
4. Emmerich, W. (2000). Software Engineering and Middleware: A Roadmap. In *Proceedings of the Conference on the Future of Software Engineering,* May 2000.
5. Bacon, J. and Moody, K. (2002). Adaptive Middleware: Toward Open, Secure, Widely Distributed Services. *Communications of the ACM, 45,* 6, June.
6. Tomasic, A. and Garcia-Molina H. (1993). Query Processing and Inverted Indices in Shared Document Retrieval Systems. *International Journal on Very Large Data Bases, 2,* 3, July.
7. Weinsberg, Y. and Ben-Shaul, I. (2002). A Programming Model and System Support for Disconnected-Aware Applications on Resource-Constrained Devices. In *Proceedings of the 24th International Conference on Software Engineering,* May 2002.
8. Guthrie, W. (1995). An Overview of Portable GUI Software. *ACM SIGCHI Bulletin, 27,* 1, January.
9. Bishop, J. and Horspool, N. (2004). Events vs. GUIs: Developing Principles of GUI Programming Using Views. In *Proceedings of the 35th SIGCSE Technical Symposium on Computer Science Education,* May 2004.
10. Qiang T., Vonderembse, M., Ragu-Nathan, T., and Ragu-Nathan, B. (2004). Measuring Modularity-Based Manufacturing Practices and Their Impact on Mass Customization Capability: A Customer-Driven Perspective. *Decision Sciences, 35,* 2, Spring.
11. Abrahams, A., Eyers, D., and Bacon J. (2002). An Asynchronous Rule-based Approach for Business Process Automation Using Obligations. In *Proceedings of the 2002 ACM SIGPLAN Workshop on Rule-based Programming,* October 2002.
12. Ranky, P., Lonkar, M., and ChamyVelumani, S. (2003). eTransition Models of Collaborating Design and Manufacturing Enterprises. *International Journal of Computer Integrated Manufacturing, 16* 4/5, June–July.

13. D'Hondt, M. and Jonckers, V. (2004). Hybrid Aspects for Weaving Object-Oriented Functionality and Rule-based Knowledge. In *Proceedings of the 3rd International Conference on Aspect-oriented Software Development,* March 2004.

14. Adelberg, B., Garcia-Molina, H., and Kao, B. (1995). Applying Update Streams in a Soft Real-time Database System. In *Proceedings of the 1995 ACM SIGMOD International Conference on Management of Data, 24,* 2, May.

15. Chen, A., Goes, P., and Marsden, J. (2002). A Query-Driven Approach to the Design and Management of Flexible Database Systems. *Journal of Management Information Systems, 19,* 3, Winter.

16. Kimball, R., Reeves, L., Ross, M., and Thornthwaite, W. (1998). *The Data Warehouse Lifecycle Toolkit.* Wiley.

17. Sammon, D. and Finnegan, P. (2000). The Ten Commandments of Data Warehousing. *ACM SIGMIS Database, 31,* 4, April.

18. HyoungDo K. (2002). Conceptual Modeling and Specification Generation for B2B Business Processes Based on ebXML. *ACM SIGMOD Record, 31,* 1, March.

19. Huemer, C. (2001). Unambiguous Access to XML-based Business Documents in B2B e-Commerce. In *Proceedings of the 3rd ACM Conference on Electronic Commerce,* October 2001.

20. Theofanos, F. and Redish, J. (2003). Guidelines for Accessible—and Usable—Web Sites. *Interactions,* X.6, November–December.

21. Bellavista, P., Corradi, A., Mntanari, R., and Stefanelli, C. (2003). Context-Aware Middleware for Resource Management in a Wireless Internet. *IEEE Transactions on Software Engineering, 29,* 12, December.

22. Tarasewich, P. (2003). Designing Mobile Commerce Applications. *Communications of the ACM, 46,* 12, December.

23. Hwang, G., Chang, S., and Chu, H. (2004). Technology for Testing Nondeterministic Client/Server Database Applications. *IEEE Transactions on Software Engineering, 30,* 1, January.

24. Melton, J. (1999). *Understanding Relational Language Components.* Morgan Kaufmann.

25. Geroimenko, V. (2004). *Dictionary of XML Technologies and the Semantic Web.* Springer-Verlag.

26. Felber, P. (2003). Sclabale Filtering of XML Data for Web Services. *IEEE Internet Computing, 7,* 1, January–February.

27. Patil, S. and Newcomer, E. (2003). ebXML and Web Services. *IEEE Internet Computing, 7,* 3, May–June.

28. Widle, E. (2003). XML Technologies Dissected. *IEEE Internet Computing, 7,* 5, September–October.

29. Dalal, S., Temel, S., Little, M., Potts, M., and Webber, J. (2003). Coordinating Business Transactions on the Web. *IEEE Internet Computing, 7,* 1, January–February.

30. Bhowmick, S., Madria, S., and Ng, W. (2004). *Web Data Management.* Springer-Verlag.

31. Gray, P., Kerschberg, L., and King, J., Poulovassilis. (2004). *The Functional Approach to Data Management.* Springer-Verlag.

32. Fensel, D. (2004). *Onotlogies.* Springer-Verlag.

33. Christensen, A., Møller, A., and Schwartzbach, M. (2003). Extending Java for High-Level Web Service Construction. *ACM Transactions on Programming Languages and Systems, 25,* 6, November.

34. Keen, A., Ge, T., Maris, J., and Olsson, R. (2004). Flexible Distributed Programming in an Extended Java Environment. *ACM Transactions on Programming Languages and Systems, 26,* 3, March.

35. Gößner, J., Mayer, P., and Steimann, F. (2004). Interface Utilization in the Java Development Kit. In *Proceedings of the 2004 ACM Symposium on Applied Computing,* March 2004.

36. Blanken, H., Grabs, T., Schek, H., Schenkel, R., and Weikum, G. (2003). *Intelligent Search on XML Data.* Springer-Verlag.

37. Bawa, J., Dorazio, P., and Trenner, L. (2001). *The Usability Business: Making the Web Work.* Springer-Verlag.

38. Baxley, B. (2003). *Making the Web Work: Designing Effective Web Applications.* New Riders Publishing.

39. Hovy, E. (2003). Using an Ontology to Simplify Data Access. *Communications of the ACM, 46,* 1, January.

40. Ghanem, T. and Aref, W. (2004). Databases Deepen the Web. *IEEE Computer, 37,* 1, January.

41. Siegel, D. (2003). The Business Case for User-Centered Design. *Interactions,* May–June.

42. Souter, A. and Pollock, L. (2003). The Construction of Contextual Def-Use Associations for Object-Oriented Systems. *IEEE Transactions on Software Engineering, 29,* 11, November.

43. Long, B., Hoffman, D., and Strooper, P. (2003). Tool Support for Testing Concurrent Java Components. *IEEE Transactions on Software Engineering, 29,* 6, June.

44. Mori, G., Paterno, F., and Santoro, C. (2004). Design and Development of Multidevice User Interfaces through Multiple Logical Descriptions. *IEEE Transactions on Software Engineering, 30,* 8, August.

45. Johnson, J. (2004). Web Bloopers: Common Web Design Mistakes and How to Avoid Them. ACM Professional Development Seminar, MIT Room 34-101, October 23, 2004.

46. Rosenberg, D. (2004). The Myths of Usability ROI. *Interactions, XI.5,* September–October.

47. Turetken, O., Schuff, D., Sharda, R., and Ow, T. (2004). Supporting Systems Analysis and Design through Fisheye Views. *Communications of the ACM, 47,* 9, September.

48. Zdun, U., Kircher, M., and Volter, M. (2004). Remoting Patterns: Design Reuse of Distributed Object Middleware Solutions. *Internet Computing, 8,* 6, November/December, 2004.

12

DATA ARCHITECTURE

Without data, computers have no business purpose. It is the information asset[21] that enables a business to correctly respond to its events. Database technology has a history of serving applications. First it served the applications that handled transactions, and then the applications that support decision making.[1] Adaptable e-commerce applications place special design constraints on data,[22] databases, and data architecture.[18] As discussed in Chapter 11, these requirements center on the need to Separate Transactional Data from Reporting Data (81). The patterns used to enable data architecture are:

84. Complete Event–Response = One Online Transaction
85. Business Functions Touch Only Transactional Databases
86. Isolate the Data Warehouse from Transactional Databases
87. Answer One Important Business Question First
88. Grow the Data Warehouse One Answer at a Time
89. Feed the Data Warehouse Automatically
90. Add Indexes to Speed Up Trend Analyses

The resulting data architecture would conceptually look like that in Figure 12. Notice how each of the Autonomous Business Functions (64) has a transactional database of its own, and how preset, timed triggers Feed the Data Warehouse Automatically (89).

HOW TO INTERPRET FRAMEWORK #12

The rapid creation of an Adaptable Business Connection (46) requires a data architecture that simultaneously optimizes transaction processing and complex reporting. This is accomplished in two physical layers.

The first layer is the online transaction processing (OLTP) layer. This layer is made up of many esoteric transactional databases that are designed to enable each autonomous business function to respond to its events. In this way, Business Functions Only Touch Transactional Databases (85). They never touch the data warehouse.

The second layer is the online analytical processing (OLAP) layer. Its purpose is to

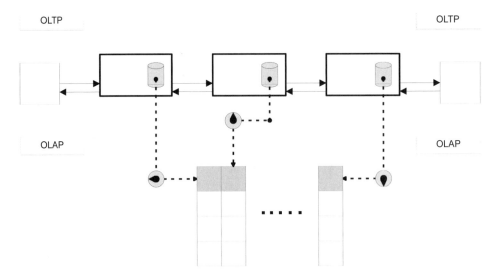

Figure 12. Framework #12: The data warehouse is isolated and fed automatically.

Isolate the Data Warehouse from Transactional Databases (86). It extracts data from the transactional databases in order to create answers to key business questions. It is strongly recommended that a company Grow the Data Warehouse One Answer at a Time (88) and take special care in understanding how to Feed the Data Warehouse Automatically (89) in order to create meaningful and timely answers.

The remainder of this chapter details each of the patterns that, together, create Framework #12.

Pattern 84. Complete Event–Response = One Online Transaction

Trust is a prerequisite for transactions.[2,3] Once trust is established, customers cause business events to happen. By considering a single event–response pair to be a unique transaction,[17] you enable each entity in the supply chain to potentially participate in that transaction.[3]

> *An online transaction is the total activity and associated data processing*
> *needed to completely detect and respond to a particular business event.*

For example, one design technique is to tag each event–response pair with its transaction type. This exploits the knowledge that exists in the entire supply chain so that any function with knowledge about a transaction type can volunteer to assist in a response by putting out a message. If a function processing that transaction type needs help, it looks for messages from volunteers.

Therefore, define transactions to be Measurable Event–Response Pairs (71). Tag each event–response pair with a transaction type to maximize cooperation. During responses, share the Common Body of Knowledge (13) across functions in order to Leverage People and Information (14).

Pattern 85. Business Functions Touch Only Transactional Databases

The knowledge that each business function has about responding to events is kept in its own transactional database,[4] designed for very fast data creation, read, update, and delete.[5] Thus, all knowledge about all transactions can, and should, be kept by each business function.[6]

> *Save the entire processing history for every transaction by letting each business function have its own (logical) transaction database.*

For example, Unlimited Storage (35) lets us keep a complete record of each transaction for future analysis (e.g., saving all time cards permits labor pricing analysis by supplier, geography, etc.). But these analyses are potentially complex, and thus must not impede the transactions. Also, permitting each function to have its own historical database of the transactions it has processed enables the e-enterprise to learn.

Therefore, save every fact and all knowledge about every transaction. Keep Transactions Separate from Decisions (63). Allow Autonomous Business Functions (64) to only have access to transactional data.

Pattern 86. Isolate the Data Warehouse from Transactional Databases

Transactional databases support online transaction processing (OLTP), and thus are optimized for speed. Their design is, thus, poor for online analytical processing (OLAP).[7,20] In fact, running analytics (i.e., reports) on OLTP data may cause serious event–response degradation.[8]

> *Create the data warehouse (OLAP) as a completely separate database entity from transactional databases (OLTP).*

For example, reports from transactional databases are difficult to write and are inefficient because these databases are constructed around hundreds of atomic business objects, each having many relationships with other objects within the context of performing transactions.

Therefore, support decision making with a data warehouse. Separate it from all transactional databases. Design it to be the authority for all reports. Ensure that All Reports Run Against the Data Warehouse (82).

Pattern 87. Answer One Important Business Question First

Data warehouses have an architecture designed to take transactional data and reorganize it for fast reporting.[9] The optimal design is a table of facts (e.g., sales, inventory units) organized around all important business dimensions (e.g., time, geography, product, customer).[8]

> *Start populating the data warehouse by answering one business question. Do not attempt to gain efficiency by combining answers.*

For example, the question, "What is monthly total labor spending for each supplier?" is answered with a table of time card charges and two separate dimension tables, one for time period (e.g., months) and one containing supplier company names. The result is a "star" architecture (with time in the middle of the star) that contains all possible answers to the question.

Therefore, start the design of your data warehouse by answering just one business question. Put "answer data" in the data warehouse fact table, and put "question data" in the data warehouse dimension tables.

Pattern 88. Grow the Data Warehouse One Answer at a Time

Business durability requires strategic planners to constantly formulate new questions[19] and obtain answers based on the latest operational data.[10] As soon as a new question is formulated, the data warehouse must be populated with the answer using data from the OLTP.[11]

> *Grow the Data Warehouse slowly, one answer at a time. Do not attempt to gain efficiency by combining answers.*

For example, given the data warehouse example in pattern #87, to answer a new question, "What is monthly total labor spending by each supplier in each state?" a new dimension table is added—a geographic table containing the names of states. Thus, the addition of a table to the existing "star" architecture enables the answer to a new question without having to do large amounts of new programming.

Therefore, add facts to the fact table and add or change dimension tables slowly. Make changes so as to answer just one new question. Use the Steering Committee (113) to control data warehouse growth.

Pattern 89. Feed the Data Warehouse Automatically

The data warehouse fact table and dimension tables are populated using OLTP "data feeds[12]." Each feed is defined, built and instituted as a corporate standard,[13] because if any feed were to change, answers from the data warehouse would become inconsistent.

> *Use only automatic (i.e., "triggered") data feeds to populate the data warehouse with real-time data. Time the feeds so they do not impede the OLTP.*

For example, the data warehouse given in pattern #88 is fed by tiny transactional database "queries," possibly timed to execute at midnight, to pull new and adjusted time card data into the fact table. New supplier names and new state names are added the night following their creation. The feeds are the only "touches" to the OLTP permitted outside the normal transactional processing.

Therefore, incrementally feed the data warehouse with data that is new or has changed since the last feed. Use "triggers" to automatically "pull" data from transactional databases at times that will not impede the OLTP.

Pattern 90. Add Indexes to Speed Up Trend Analyses

Consider the data warehouse to be a collection of full or partially computed answers to key business questions.[15] Once its answers have been methodically designed, built, and retrieved,[16] data warehouse performance can be optimized[17] using a technique called "indexing."

> *When needed, add indexes to one or more answers to enable reporting*
> *queries and trend analysis queries to perform better.*

For example, reports are almost always constrained by time. Also, incremental data feeds populate the data warehouse within a given "time window." Therefore, time is almost always the first index created. Thus, it is common to see time in the center of a star-like data warehouse.

Therefore, carefully study data warehouse performance and make a plan before creating indexes. Use "date" as the primary index key on the fact table. Create one unique index for each large dimension table.

IMPLICATIONS OF PATTERN USE

An Adaptable e-Business Connection (46) requires an adaptable data architecture, designed first and foremost to Isolate the Data Warehouse from Transactional Databases (86). In addition:

- From a transactional perspective, your data design should center around two factors: (a) that a Complete Event–Response = One Online Transaction (84), and (b) that the data architecture ensures that all Business Functions Touch Only Transactional Databases (85).

- From a data warehouse perspective, your data design should concentrate on two primary factors: (a) a data warehouse is built by a method that will Answer One Important Business Question First (87), and (b) you should Grow the Data Warehouse One Answer at a Time (88).

The data warehouse is populated by software triggers that Feed the Data Warehouse Automatically (89). A separate design concern, which should be addressed after initial data warehouse population, is its performance. Optimization occurs via a technique to incrementally Add Indexes to Speed Up Trend Analyses (90). Additionally, if an autonomous business function requires particular data that must come from the data warehouse, that data should be generated ahead of time (within the required freshness cycle), and made available via other special autonomous functions.

REFERENCES

1. Jhingran, A. (2000). Supporting e-Commerce Applications on Databases. *ACM SIGMOD Record, 29,* 4, December.
2. Salam, A., Rao, H., and Pegels C. (2003). Virtual Extension: Consumer-Perceived Risk in e-Commerce Transactions. *Communications of the ACM, 46,* 12, December.
3. Elliman, T. and Orange, G. (2003). Developing Distributed Design Capabilities in the Construction Supply Chain. *Construction Innovation, 3,* 1, March.

4. Garcia-Molina, H. (1983). Using Semantic Knowledge for Transaction Processing in a Distributed Database. *ACM Transactions on Database Systems, 8,* 2, June.

5. Abiteboul, S. and Vianu V. (1989). A Transaction-based Approach to Relational Database Specification. *Journal of the ACM, 36,* 4, October.

6. Traiger, I., Gray, J., Galtieri, C., and Lindsay, B. (1982). Transactions and Consistency in Distributed Database Systems. *ACM Transactions on Database Systems, 7,* 3, September.

7. Simon, A., Shaffer, S., and Goethals, F. (2001). *Data Warehousing and Business Intelligence for e-Commerce.* Morgan Kaufman.

8. Kimbal, R., Reeves, L., Ross, M., and Thornthwaite, W. (1998). *The Data Warehouse Life Cycle Toolkit.* Wiley.

9. Hoven, J. (2003). Data Architecture Principles for Data. *Information Systems Management, 20,* 3, Summer.

10. Srinivasan, N. and Balasubramanian, G. (2003). Strategic Thinking: A Neuronal Architectural View. *Vikalpa: The Journal for Decision Makers, 28,* 4, October–December.

11. Chan, M., Va Leong, H., and Si, A. (2000). Incremental Update to Aggregated Information for Data Warehouses over the Internet. In *Proceedings of the 3rd ACM International Workshop on Data Warehousing and OLAP,* November 2000.

12. Roodyn, N. and Emmerich, W. (1999). An Architectural Style for Multiple Real-time Data Feeds. In *Proceedings of the 21st International Conference on Software Engineering,* May 1999.

13. Gardner, S. (1998). Building the Data Warehouse. *Communications of the ACM, 41,* 9, September.

14. de Souza, M. and Sampaio, M. (1999). Efficient Materialization and Use of Views in Data Warehouses. *ACM SIGMOD Record, 28,* 1, March.

15. Nascimento, M. and Dunham, M. (1996). Indexing a Transaction-Decision Time Database. In *Proceedings of the 1996 ACM Symposium on Applied Computing,* February 1996.

16. Winter, R. and Strauch, B. (2004). Information Requirements Engineering for Data Warehouse Systems. In *Proceedings of the 2004 ACM Symposium on Applied Computing,* March 2004.

17. Cleland-Hang, J., Chang, C., and Christensen, M. (2003). Event-Based Traceability for Managing Evolutionary Change. *IEEE Transactions on Software Engineering, 29,* 9., September.

18. Evernden, R. and Evernden, E. (2003). Third-Generation Information Architecture. *Communications of the ACM, 46,* 3, March.

19. Menzies, T. and Hu, Y. Data Mining for Very Busy People. *IEEE Computer, 36,* 11, November.

20. Gorla, N. (2003). Features to Consider in a Data Warehousing System. *Communications of the ACM, 46,* 11, November.

21. Holmes, N. (2004). Data and Information as Property. *IEEE Computer, 37,* 5, May.

22. Park, J. and Ram, S. (2004). Information Systems Interoperability: What Lies Beneath? *ACM Transactions on Information Systems, 22,* 4, October.

IV

e-PROJECT

To accomplish an e-project (plan, specify, design, build, and deploy an adaptive e-enterprise solution), concentrate on managing its complexity:

- Create a management framework (Chapter 13) for fully defining the solution before its construction, and for tightly managing all the implementation and deployment efforts.
- Follow formal project management (Chapter 14) to control changes to the plan and the e-business process, and to proactively oversee the integration of technologies among companies.
- Practice implementation management (Chapter 15) by adhering to a comprehensive set of e-business implementation methodologies.
- Develop a team management (Chapter 16) approach, using the concept of a tightly connected set of highly specialized subteams.

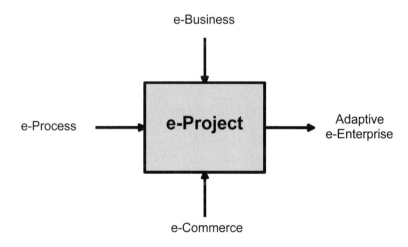

13

MANAGEMENT FRAMEWORK

e-business projects now absorb more of the IT budget,[1] so firms are using disciplined programs to implement these initiatives,[2] especially through enterprise project management.[3,40] e-business project success requires balancing imagination and methodology[4] while providing tight coordination among many the participating organizations to reduce risk.[5,44,46] For contract labor management, project timelines are often short and fixed, requirements change must be controlled,[41] project focus is on the outsourcing agreement, and implementation requires heavy coordination, single point of control, and external oversight. For these reasons, an e-project relies heavily on a management framework and employs these patterns:

91. Project Constraints and Assumptions
92. Solid Project Definition
93. Comprehensive Project Team
94. Accurate and Controlled Estimates
95. Tight Project Control
96. Project Repository
97. Proactive Project Oversight

The resulting e-project management framework would conceptually look like the one in Figure 13. Notice that the e-project constraints and assumptions are the factors that impinge on the project. They, and any other factors that contribute to project complexity, are the elements that will require great deal of management attention. Hence, a management framework, an online project repository, and constant oversight, are all essential.

HOW TO INTERPRET FRAMEWORK #13

Due to its complexity and scope, an e-project must utilize a predefined management framework in order to maximize the chance of its success.

Project Constraints and Assumptions (91) are defined and approved often before a Solid Project Definition (92) is completed. The e-project definition includes a Comprehen-

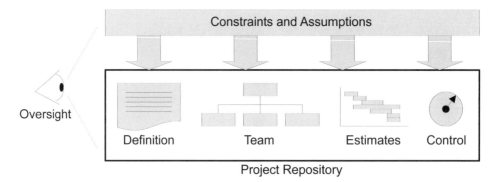

Figure 13. Framework #13: An e-project framework to manage complexity.

sive Project Team (93) that identifies all executive and key stakeholder parties. After definition and prior to execution, an e-project plan is created. This plan comprises a complete work breakdown structure, having Accurate and Controlled Estimates (94). Tight Project Control (95) is achieved by maintaining, minute by minute, all project information in a central Project Repository (96) and using that information during Proactive Project Oversight (97) activities. These activities occur at regularly scheduled times. Hourly, daily, weekly, and monthly time periods may all be required.

The remainder of this chapter details each of the patterns that, together, create Framework #13.

Pattern 91. Project Constraints and Assumptions

Successful e-business projects keep a close watch on the risk factors,[47] especially the constraints and assumptions.[6] Part of this monitoring requires an analysis of project atmosphere, stakeholders,[38] and centers of influence.[7] And because of the enterprise-wide nature of the project, the CIO has a distinct role in surfacing assumptions early.[8]

> *Prior to e-project planning, define all project constraints and assumptions, plus methods for monitoring them.*

For example, a project schedule is finalized by allocating personnel according to "ramp-up" constraints and assumptions. After all sponsors and stakeholders agree to that plan, the ramp up is tracked very closely (sometimes hourly!) to immediately identify any risks to the schedule. It is the risk, more than the schedule, that must be managed on an e-project.

Therefore, keep definitions for all Project Constraints and Assumptions (91) in the Project Repository (96). Ensure that Proactive Project Oversight (97) includes the constant monitoring of constraints and assumptions.

Pattern 92. Solid Project Definition

Project risk[49] is lessened with solid, up-front planning[9] that produces a project approach aligned to corporate objectives,[10] a comprehensive work breakdown structure (WBS)[11,12] and resource plan,[13] defined control points,[14] and a complete set of expected communications.[15]

> *Define an e-Project so everyone clearly understands its goal, scope, approach, personnel, timeframe, cost, and ROI.*

For example, a successful contract labor outsourcing plan includes project scope, strategy, structure, team roster and ramp up, success measures, and all required communications to the stakeholders. It is not just a project schedule with deliverables. It is comprehensive in scope.

Therefore, create a Solid Project Definition (92) and keep it in the Project Repository (96). Refer to it especially during transition between Formal Project Stages (98), during Project Plan Management (100), and during Business Relationship Management (103).

Pattern 93. Comprehensive Project Team

e-business pressures projects to create a cohesive,[16] interdisciplinary[17] team, and pressures project managers to be flexible in light of the large number of project stakeholders.[18,38] Also, the team must attend to its relationship with the organization,[48] and to how well it manages itself.[19]

> *Build a comprehensive e-project team. Assign one person to each project area. Include all organizational stakeholders.*

For example, contract labor outsourcing projects typically have dozens of stakeholders from HR, procurement, engineering, and manufacturing. They also include team leads, each of which is responsible for the program office, the supply chain, the technology, the data, and so on. Assigning one responsible person to each project area solidifies the plan.

Therefore, invest in building a Comprehensive Project Team (93) and training project personnel in Highly Coordinated Teamwork (99). Use a Project Team Framework (112) to cover all critical project areas.

Pattern 94. Accurate and Controlled Estimates

A successful project refines its estimates.[20,45] Proposal estimates have a ±100% accuracy. Early planning estimates have a ±25% accuracy. Deliverable estimates have a ±5% accuracy. Good project managers maintain strong control over estimates[21] by reviewing them weekly with the project team, and reviewing them daily as the project nears deployment.

> *Thoroughly define and control all e-project estimates. Provide accuracy ranges (plus or minus a percentage point) in order to correctly set expectations.*

For example, a prematurely exact figure incorrectly sets expectations. Instead, whenever possible, provide estimate ranges—project phases first, project milestones second, and actual deliverables third. If the project end date is fixed, then you must relax either scope or cost. Without the ability to relax one of the three, your project will likely fail.[49]

Therefore, exercise Tight Project Control (95) via Accurate and Controlled Estimates

(94). Use formal Project Plan Management (100) whenever an agreed-upon estimate must change.

Pattern 95. Tight Project Control

Tight control is accomplished via a project plan in which estimates are fixed.[21] This "baseline" plan is a visual control[22] that enables regular evaluations[23] to show progress, to identify variations,[24] and to compute ROI.[25,26] Without a baseline, project status reverts to people's opinions, which too often are overly optimistic and lack grounding in reality.

> *Establish a plan baseline by "freezing" all deliverables and their due dates.*
> *Use a baseline to track progress and assess risk.*

For example, contract labor outsourcing projects are managed tightly to the "go live" date defined in the master service agreement, and to any crucial intermediate due dates such as a project's major phases. Once the plan is agreed on, these dates are fixed (i.e., the so-called "baselining" of the project plan) so they can be tracked.

Therefore, use only a plan baseline to achieve Tight Project Control (95). Once defined, never relax or change the controls. Use these controls during Proactive Project Oversight (97).

Pattern 96. Project Repository

The nature of e-business projects requires them to constantly provide information to their teams.[27,28] This is best accomplished via a Web-based portal[29] that gives people easy access to a project repository[30,37] that contains, in one location,[42] all up-to-the-minute information[31] and project management tools[32] for concentrated team problem solving.

> *Build and maintain a project repository with up-to-the-minute information*
> *and the latest tools. Make its access and use very easy.*

For example, a project repository for a contract labor outsourcing effort includes the project plan and its deliverables and baselines, commodity pricing analyses, and all contracts, policies, forms, and procedures. Every piece of information regarding how the outsourcing was designed and the intentions behind how it should operate are put in the repository.

Therefore, populate the Project Repository (96) with Project Constraints and Assumptions (91), the Solid Project Definition (92), Accurate and Controlled Estimates (94), and any up-to-the-minute information that can affect these elements. Also include all project management tools.

Pattern 97. Proactive Project Oversight

e-Business project managers and CIOs[33] proactively assess risk[34] such as organizational resistance, integration complexity,[39] and resource unavailability. They monitor solution compliance[43] to expected policies, process, workflow, and data.[35] Often, oversight of strategy, process, and information means the difference between success and failure.[36]

Proactively monitor all known project risks and periodically attempt to identify unknown risks. If needed, dedicate additional resources to this crucial task.

For example, a project manager for a contract labor outsourcing effort must be aware daily of the Value Chain Transition (106) so that neither suppliers nor stakeholders communicate incorrectly about the project. The act of managing project expectations relies on accurate and timely information, as well as an analysis of how that information might be interpreted. This activity is complex and may require its own subproject.

Therefore, make Proactive Project Oversight (97) the job of everyone on the Comprehensive Project Team (93). Use methods for Tight Project Control (95) to assess Project Constraints and Assumptions (91) and validate the Accurate and Controlled Estimates (94).

IMPLICATIONS OF PATTERN USE

When an Adaptable e-Business Connection (46) has a wide scope and is technically, socially, or politically complex, its corresponding e-project must use a very distinct management framework:

- At e-project formulation, the management framework helps people define Project Constraints and Assumptions (91), develop a Solid Project Definition (92), and create a Comprehensive Project Team (93).
- During e-project planning, the management framework helps people create Accurate and Controlled Estimates (94) for the entire project plan and for any of its subplans.
- During e-project execution, the management framework calls for Tight Project Control (95) and Proactive Project Oversight (97). It requires all project information and tools to reside in a Project Repository (96).

Therefore, the management framework becomes a tool that is used throughout the e-project to manage complexity. In other words, the ultimate priority for the project manager is to manage complexity. This priority differs from traditional projects in which the primary objective is to mange schedule and cost. It is still critical to manage schedule and cost on an e-project, but the complexity factors can, at any time, quickly surface and overwhelm any schedule and cost concerns. This is why it is recommended that every e-project consider whether it should have a project management team, not just an individual, for risk management.

REFERENCES

1. Chung, A. (2003). By the Numbers: Tight Pocketbooks Find Room for e-Business. *Baseline,* Issue 023, October.
2. Selig, G. (2003). Strategic Enterprise Initiatives—From Strategy to Implementation for Executives. In *Project World Seminar,* Boston, MA, June 2003.
3. Bigelow, D. (2004). The Future is EPM. *PM Network, 18,* 4, April.

4. Tiwana, A. and McLean, E. (2003). Virtual Extension: The Tightrope to e-Business Project Success. *Communications of the ACM, 46,* 12, December.

5. Kalakota, R. and Whinston, A. (1996). *Frontiers of Electronic Commerce.* Addison-Wesley.

6. Raz, T., Barnes, R., and Dvir, D. (2003). A Critical Look at Critical Chain Project Management. *Project Management Journal. 34,* 4, December.

7. Kayed, O. (2003). Seven Steps to Dynamic Scope Design. *PM Network, 17,* 12, December.

8. Potter, R. (2003). How CIOs Manage their Superior's Expectations. *Communications of the ACM, 46,* 8, August.

9. Foti, R. (2004). Expect the Unexpected. *PM Network, 18,* 7, July.

10. Kayed, O. (2003). Seven Steps to Dynamic Scope Design. *M Network, 17,* 12, December.

11. PMI. (2004). *Practice Standard for Work Breakdown Structures.* Project Management Institute Press.

12. Haugan, G. (2004). *Effective Work breakdown Structures.* Project Management Institute Press.

13. Callahan, K. and Brooks, L. (2003). Creating a Project Charter. In *Project World Seminar,* Boston, MA, June 2003.

14. Chauduri, T. and Schlotzhauer, D. (2003). So Many Projects, So Little Time. *PM Network, 17,* 10, October.

15. Atkins, S. and Gilbert, G. (2003). The Role of Induction and Training in Team Effectivness. *Project Management Journal, 34,* 2, June.

16. Mullaly, M. (2003). Co-operation, Collaboration & Conflict: Insights into Managing Great Teams. In *Project World Seminar,* Boston, MA, June 2003.

17. Anonymous. (2000). Chase-ing e-Business. *IIE Solutions, 32,* 6, June.

18. Essex, D. (2003). e-Business Boom. *PM Network, 17,* 3, March.

19. Chan, S. (2000). E-commerce Workforce Development Strategies: A Dialogue with Industry. In *Proceedings of the 2000 ACM SIGCPR Conference on Computer Personnel Research,* April 2000.

20. Keane. (1995). *Productivity Management.* Keane, Inc.

21. Coombs, P. (2003). *IT Project Estimation.* Cambridge University Press.

22. Greif, M. (2002). *The Visual Factory.* Productivity Press.

23. Jackson, L. (2004). Forge Ahead. *PM Network, 18,* 4, April.

24. DeWeaver, M. and Gillespie, L. (2002). *Real-World Project Management.* Productivity Press.

25. Anonymous. (2002). e-Business: Finding the ROI. *ABA Banking Journal, Supplement, 94,* 11, November.

26. Cronin, M. (1996). *The Internet Strategy Handbook.* Harvard Business School Press.

27. Cone, E. (2003). Divide & Conquer. *Baseline,* Issue 015, February.

28. Tiwana, A. and McLean, E. (2002). Virtual Work and Teams: Knowledge Integration and Individual Expertise Development in e-Business Project Teams. In *Proceedings of the 2002 ACM SIGCPR Conference on Computer Personnel Research,* May 2002.

29. Patterson, D. (2004). Promote Your Project Management Portal for Better Staff Buy-In. *PM Network, 18,* 5, May.

30. Frank, L. (2004). On Demand. *PM Network, 18,* 4, April.

31. Ingebretsen, M. (2003). Enter the War Room. *PM Network, 17,* 5, May.

32. Hallows, J. (2004). *The Oroject Management Office Toolkit.* Project Management Institute Press.

33. Potter, R. (2003). How CIOs Manage their Superior's Expectations. *Communications of the ACM, 46,* 8, August.

34. Foti, R. (2004). Expect the Unexpected. *PM Network, 18,* 7, July.

35. Ash, C. and Burn J. (2001). m-Powering Personnel for e-Business Change. In *Proceedings of the 2001 ACM SIGCPR Conference on Computer Personnel Research,* April 2001.

36. Boulton, R., Libert, B., and Samek, S. (2000). *Cracking the Value Code.* HarperCollins.

37. Jantunen, A. (2004). Knowledge Management and Quality of People for Enduring Competitive Dominance. In *Proceedings of 13th International Conference for the Management of Technology,* April 2004.

38. Oschadleus, J. (2004). Communicate to Influence: Managing Project Stakeholders and Team Members. In *Proceedings of PMI Seminar,* Orlando, Florida, June, 2004.

39. Xia, W. and Lee, G. (2004). Grasping the Complexity of IS Development Projects. *Communications of the ACM, 47,* 5, May.

40. Dinsmore, P. (2003). Winning in Business with Enterprise Project Management. In *Proceedings of PMI Seminar,* Dallas, Texas, October 2003.

41. Armitage, J. (2004). Are Agile Methods Good for Design? *Interactions,* January–February.

42. Abraham, D. and Chen, S. (2003). A Framework for Knowledge Management Processes in Professional Services Organizations. In *CCCT'03 Proceedings,* August 2003.

43. Basili, V., Shull, F., and Lanubile, F. (1999). Building Knowledge through Families of Experiments. *IEEE Transactions on Software Engineering, 25,* 4, July–August.

44. Stern, G. (2004). Course Correction. *PM Network, 18,* 9, September.

45. PMI. (2004). *Organizational Project Management Maturity Model (OPM3®).* Project Management Institute.

46. PMI. (1991). *Project and Program Risk Management.* Project Management Institute.

47. Pinto, J. and Millet, I. (1999). *Successful Information System Implementation.* Project Management Institute.

48. Whitten, N. (2000). *The EnterPrize Organization: Organizing Software Projects for Accountability and Success.* Project Management Institute.

49. Tiwana, A. and Keil, M. (2004). The One-Minute Risk Assessment Tool. *Communications of the ACM, 47,* 11, November.

14

PROJECT MANAGEMENT

Some companies consider e-business initiatives to be very similar to traditional software development efforts.[1] So, some e-business solutions are pressed into service with insufficient capability or usability. However, some companies recognize that e-business initiatives require more than the traditional planning, requirements, design, and testing activities common to other software efforts.[24] They recognize that an e-project must use management techniques from initiatives that have varying degrees of uncertainty and organizational impact,[2] strategy implementations, for example. And because of the high visibility and wide impact of an e-project, these companies also adopt structured and disciplined[3] quality and learning methods to lessen project rework.[4] In short, they institute five additional key management patterns:

    98. Formal Project Stages
    99. Highly Coordinated Project Team
  100. Project Plan Management
  101. Process Change Management
  102. Technology Integration Management

The resulting project management framework would conceptually look like the one in Figure 14. The framework is organized into three stages: definition, implementation, and deployment. Typically, each stage will receive equal up-front investment and ongoing management attention. It is also very important to note here that if an e-project has phases, the three project stages are applied to each phase.

HOW TO INTERPRET FRAMEWORK #14

Due to its complexity and scope, an e-project is formally organized and conducted in order to maximize the chance of its success. During its definition, an e-project is sometimes broken into several phases. The objective of each phase is to accomplish one business goal. Each phase is typically broken into several Formal Project Stages (98). Since the e-project team is often large, with a high number of specialists, management practices need to define, reinforce, and support tight coordination among all team members.

Stage One	Stage Two	Stage Three
• Due Dilligence	• Solution Development	• Solution Deployment
• Steering Committee	• Co-Project Managers	• Paired Efforts
• Project Planning	• Tracking & Reporting	• Project Control
• As-Is Process	• To-Be Process	• Impact Analysis
• Connection Points	• Data Standards	• Data Loading

Figure 14. Framework #14: Three distinct stages per project or project phase.

During its execution, an e-project invests in formal Project Plan Management (100), in which the project plan is reviewed at least weekly by key parties. Any changes to the project plan are done via a change control process that also includes notification of all interested parties. Due to its process nature, e-project execution also requires tight management of process changes to minimize process variations. When an e-project has a number of interrelated technical components, it must also tightly manage each integration point between components.

The remainder of this chapter details each of the patterns that, together, create Framework #14.

Pattern 98. Formal Project Stages

Especially for e-projects, the project manager must work against the tendency to over-complicate the project's straightforward aspects.[5] An effective practice is to define formal project stages.[6] Each stage is an objective that focuses people and represents a formal control point for baselining the plan, reviewing project progress, and approving the project go-ahead.

> *During or right after project scope development, define project stages that will focus people and act as distinct control points.*

For example, contract labor outsourcing projects require three stages: due diligence (solution definition), solution development (design and build), and solution deployment (data transfer, training, and cutover). The three stages isolate project concerns and create natural signoff points.

Therefore, create distinct project stages that separate due diligence, development, and deployment. Use them to ensure Tight Project Control (95) and to allow for formal Project Plan Management (100).

Pattern 99. Highly Coordinated Teamwork

Due to its enterprise-wide scope and large number of stakeholders,[7,22] an e-project requires its team to be cohesive[8] and very efficient in how it functions.[9] Common practices include codesign, adhering to a system development life cycle, daily coordination meetings, project execution oversight, and personnel dedicated to the project repository.[10]

> *Invest time and resources in project oversight, daily coordination, adherence to development standards, and project information maintenance.*

For example, daily coordination meetings start when a contract labor outsourcing initiative shifts to deployment. They ensure each cutover task (e.g., supplier transition, data conversion) is performed exactly on time. At this point in the project, weekly status reporting cycles are ineffective.

Therefore, dedicate people and dollars to create an environment for Highly Coordinated Teamwork (99). Invest in a Project Repository (96), Tight Project Controls (95), and formal Project Plan Management (100).

Pattern 100. Project Plan Management

When the e-business and its value chain are highly complementary, strong e-project plan management is required.[11] Such management requires formal change control of project scope, strategy, and stages. It also requires meetings to ensure conformance to plan, reviews of all project plan changes, and formal end-of-stage project signoffs.[21]

> *Institute formal practices to control changes to the project, to the plan, and to how the team must execute the plan.*

For example, successful contract labor outsourcing projects typically have highly granular plans, which enable accurate weekly tracking, thorough end-of-stage reviews, and visibility of all changes of the plan.

Therefore, conduct Proactive Project Oversight (97) and use formal practices to ensure team conformance to the original Solid Project Definition (92) and to all Accurate and Controlled Estimates (94).

Pattern 101. Process Change Management

e-business operational complexity[12] and scope[13] require definition of process improvement prior to project initiation.[14] The resulting process map[15,23] must span the entire workflow, including the whole supply chain.[16] Although process relocation to gain efficiency[17,18,25] often occurs, care must also be taken to dramatically decrease process variation.[19]

> *Tightly manage process change across the value chain to reduce overall cycle time without adding process variation.*

For example, contract labor outsourcing initiatives strive to build one seamless process to fulfill orders. Fair order distribution and very fast candidate submittals are two required performance objectives. Often, it is effective process design that enables the satisfaction of such objectives.

Therefore, use formal practices to formally define, and control changes to, the Adaptable e-Business Connection. Stay true to the Outsourced Process (16) design, and to decisions that Add Value to Suppliers (15).

Pattern 102. Technology Integration Management

Since e-business is highly visible, its errors have strong competitive implications1. In addition, technology integration is currently difficult to get correct.[20,26] Thus, extra planning, design, and oversight should go into both sell-side and buy-side technology integration activities.[18]

> *Overengineer all technology integration points for transaction capture*
> *(ERP), knowledge maintenance (CRM), and trend analysis (data*
> *warehouse).*

For example, the technology component of a contract labor outsourcing effort is often implemented in phases. Three phases are common. Phase I implements new policies and processes. Phase II implements orders and related transactions. Phase III implements invoicing and payment.

Therefore, make Technology Integration Management (102) decisions part of the initial project strategy. Phase the e-project to add process value early while concurrently working on technology integration. Use Formal Project Stages (98) for each technology integration effort.

IMPLICATIONS OF PATTERN USE

When an Adaptable e-Business Connection (46) has a wide scope and is technically, socially, or politically complex, its e-project must use a more formal set of management practices:

- Formal Project Stages (98) of due diligence, solution development, and solution deployment should be strictly followed to enable Tight Project Control (95) and Proactive Project Oversight (97) from the project sponsor and from its Steering Committee (113).
- The Steering Committee (113) should invest in a Highly Coordinated Project Team (99). It should be an advocate for project comanagement and for paired expertise between the outsourcing company and the firm that will assume responsibility for the Outsourced Process (16).
- The Steering Committee (113) should also invest in formal management that is concentrated at an e-project's points of highest risk. These points are: Project Plan Management (100), Process Change Management (101), and Technology Integration Management (102).

Finally, even if an e-project has a short timeframe, the aforementioned management practices must be followed. The scope and complexity of e-projects makes them extremely vulnerable to a large number of active or potential complexity factors that could set the project back or derail it. Many of these factors, especially political ones, are not always "out in the open" and require time and attention to identify them and to develop a subsequent course of action to either remove them or mitigate them. Therefore, it is prudent to always following an effective set of management practices, regardless of project length or size. In addition, having sufficient project management resources to properly accomplish risk management is a must.

REFERENCES

1. Rayport, J. and Jaworski, B. (2003). *Introduction to e-Commerce.* McGraw-Hill.

2. Kenny, J. (2003). Effective Project Management for Strategic Innovation and Change in an Organizational Context. *Project Management Journal, 34,* 1, March.

3. Selig, G. (2003). Strategic Enterprise Initiatives—From Strategy to Implementation for Executives. In *Project World Seminar,* Boston, MA, June 2003.

4. Chung, A. (2003). By the Numbers: Tight Pocketbooks Find Room for e-Business. *Baseline,* Issue 023, October.

5. Peters, T. (2004). Fix the Spreadsheet. *PM Network, 18,* 1, January.

6. Callahan, K. and Brooks, L. (2003). Creating a Project Charter. In *Project World Seminar,* Boston, MA, June 2003.

7. Essex, D. (2003). e-Business Boom. *PM Network, 17,* 3, March.

8. Mullaly, M. (2003). Co-operation, Collaboration and Conflict: Insights into Managing Great Teams. In *Project World Seminar,* Boston, MA, June 2003.

9. Foti, R. (2003). PMI 2002 Project of the Year. *PM Network, 17,* 1, January.

10. Desouza, K. and Evaristo, R. (2004). Managing Knowledge in Distributed Projects. *Communications of the ACM, 47,* 4, April.

11. Pinker, E., Seidmann, A., and Foster, R. (2002). Strategies for Transitioning "Old Economy" Firms to e-Business. *Communications of the ACM, 45,* 5, May.

12. Morecroft, J. and Sterman, J. (2001). *Modeling for Learning Organizations.* Productivity Press.

13. Badir, Y., Founou, R., Stricker, C., and Bourquin, V. (2003). Management of Global Large-Scale Projects through a Federation of Multiple Web-Based Workflow Management Systems. *Project Management Journal, 34,* 3, September.

14. Ferraro, J. (2003). Begin with the End. *PM Network, 17,* 2, February.

15. Damelio, R. (2002). *The Basics of Process Mapping.* Productivity Press.

16. Kayed, O. (2003). Seven Steps to Dynamic Scope Design. *PM Network, 17,* 12, December.

17. Hammer, M. (2001). The Superefficient Company. *Harvard Business Review,* September.

18. Whitehead Mann Group. (2002). The I-builders. *The Economist,* March 7.

19. Edelson, N. and Bennett, C. (2002). *Process Discipline.* Productivity Press.

20. Plant, R. (2003). *e-Commerce Formulation of Strategy.* Safari Tech Books Online.

21. Krishna, R. (2004). User Acceptance Testing Heuristics for Success. In *International Conference on Software Testing,* May 2004.

22. Oschadleus, J. (2004). Communicate to Influence: Managing Project Stakeholders and Team Members. In *PMI Seminar,* Orlando, FL, June, 2004.

23. Becker, J., Kugeler, M. and Rosemann, M. (2003). *Process Management.* Springer-Verlag.

24. Xia, W. and Lee, G. (2004). Grasping the Complexity of IS Development Projects. *Communications of the ACM, 47,* 5, May.

25. Krovi, R., Chandra, A. and Rajagopalan, B. (2003). Information Flow Parameters for Managing Organizational Processes. *Communications of the ACM, 46,* 2, February.

26. Takakuwa, S., Tuzuki, T., and Matsui, K. (2003). Prototype Procurement System for Raw materials Based on MRP. In *CCCT'03 Proceedings,* August 2003.

27. Stensrud, E. and Myrtveit, I. (2003). Identifying High Performance ERP Projects. *IEEE Transactions on Software Engineering, 29,* 5, May.

15

IMPLEMENTATION MANAGEMENT

Instituting a management framework and formal management practices will help alleviate some common e-project mistakes such as unsupportive champions, unclear strategy, conflicting priorities, and poor coordination.[1] However, a comprehensive set of implementation practices[2] is also needed to create a complete, correct and usable e-business solution. This includes all the e-project communications[3] patterns:

103. Business Relationship Management
104. Commodity Pricing
105. Program Office Formulation
106. Value Chain Transition
107. Business Process Reengineering
108. Technology Configuration and Integration
109. Operational Data Transition
110. Project Communications
111. End User Training

The resulting solution implementation management framework would conceptually look like the one in Figure 15. It shows that implementation management for an e-project is very often the management of several complex initiatives happening in parallel. For example, Business Relationship Management (103) drives the entire e-project, often with two dozen Project Communications (110) occurring throughout the effort.

HOW TO INTERPRET FRAMEWORK #15

Due to its complexity and scope, an e-project must institute formal practices to minimize the occurrence of common project mistakes.

Business Relationship Management (103) is required to ensure that the desired Adaptable e-Business Connection (46) is built correctly for the desired relationship. Complete Commodity Pricing (104) definition and Program Office Formulation (105) are required

Business Relationship Management		
Commodity Pricing	Value Chain Transition	
Program Office Formulation	Business Process Reengineering	End User Training
Technology Config. & Integration	Operational Data Transition	
Project Communications		

Figure 15. Framework #15: Concurrent management of several subprojects.

prior to initiating any Value Chain Transition (106) activities. Practices for Business Process Reengineering (107), Technology Configuration and Integration (108), and Operational Data Transition (109) must all dovetail into each other. Clear and timely Project Communications (110) are also a must, as is solid End User Training (111).

The remainder of this chapter details each of the patterns that, together, create Framework #15.

Pattern 103. Business Relationship Management

The structure of the business relationship[39] is the key to correct e-business design.[4] This may include service expansion,[5] outsourcing strategy,[6] and master contract negotiation.[7] Thus, a dedicated team should be devoted to this area. They should also define the steering committee, the business issue escalation path, and the communication plan.

> *Define the business relationship before initiating the e-project. Proactively maintain all aspects of that definition during the project.*

For example, contract labor outsourcing efforts always dedicate people to the Master Agreement (18), Steering Committee (113) formulation, outsourcing strategy, and issue escalation process. Wise executives know that without a full definition of the intended business relationship, some circumstance always arises to put the relationship in jeopardy.

Therefore, create a Business Relationship Team (114) to define and maintain the business relationship. Make sure the Outsourced Process (16) and Adaptable e-Business Connection (46) match the relationship.

Pattern 104. Commodity Pricing

e-Enterprise solutions that seek savings usually invest in commodity price benchmarking.[11] Although Internet technology opens the door to real-time pricing, which may increase savings,[12] a benchmark[36] that levels the playing field without adding cost to suppliers is desired.[13]

*Follow a methodology to develop a commodity pricing schedule that treats
all suppliers fairly, regardless of tier.*

For example, contract labor outsourcing efforts usually benchmark labor across the entire geography of the outsourcing firm. They first scrub the current invoices, then identify price anomalies in skill set or geography, and, finally, develop savings recommendations. They also identify esoteric manager-to-supplier agreements that yield no value.

Therefore, create a subproject to develop Commodity Pricing (104). Analyze current Skill Niches (22) and Supplier Subtiers (24) to form a Standard Pricing Table (23) that yields savings and is fair to all suppliers.

Pattern 105. Program Office Formulation

The hub-and-spoke design, with price as the decision-making variable, is common in e-business design.[8] At the hub is the program office, whose job is to ensure overall process efficiency without sacrificing quality.[9] But the program office needs to be strategic as well as tactical.[10]

*Design and build a program office that will proactively manage the value
chain, both strategically and tactically.*

For example, a contract labor management program office manages suppliers to the program's performance metrics, and performs resource planning with those managers who need to place orders in the future due to up-coming major initiatives. Such services add enormous value.

Therefore, create a Program Office Team (115) to define and manage all the rules of the Adaptable e-Business Connection (46). Make sure they follow all Business Relationship Management (103) practices. Give them highly personalized End User Rraining (111).

Pattern 106. Value Chain Transition

The supply chain's growing influence on the bottom line[14] demands new ways of e-sourcing.[15] Thus, value chain demand, flow, and leveling analyses,[16] which seek to identify variability and optimize cycle time, are now being formally included in e-business initiatives.

*Follow a methodology to analyze the value chain, identify effective
suppliers, and transition those suppliers into the new e-business.*

For example, contract labor outsourcing efforts typically transition current suppliers via interviews, qualification, subcontract negotiation, and "on-boarding." This process emphasizes fairness across the supply base.

Therefore, analyze the entire Value Chain (25), including all Supplier Subtiers (24). Identify those suppliers likely to adhere to the new Commodity Pricing (104) and Performance Metrics (21), and transition each of those into the e-business solution by using a standard method.

Pattern 107. Business Process Reengineering

Many companies have already reengineered their core supply chain process.[14] They sought overall cycle time reduction[18] with minimal process variation.[19] But when processes are still complex, inefficient,[38] outdated, redundant, or burdensome,[20] they are very costly.[21]

> *Give your e-project time to methodically assess the supply chain process,*
> *even if it has just been reengineered. Focus on overall cost.*

For example, contract labor outsourcing efforts thoroughly assess each step in the end-to-end process: requisition, fulfillment, payroll, invoicing, and payment. Assessment results also help in technology integration efforts.

Therefore, assess the current Value Chain (25) process against the intended Outsourced Process (16). Focus on cost, response, and simplicity. Identify needed process changes and associated Process Change Management (101), and factor these into the e-project plan.

Pattern 108. Technology Configuration and Integration

Business survival now relies on e-business. Companies must become more transparent and must put the right technical infrastructure in place.[14] But infrastructure transition is most often successful when it is iterative (gradual) as opposed to reengineered (radical).[22]

> *Follow a methodology that configures and integrates technology so that*
> *infrastructure transition occurs smoothly. Avoid radical replacement of*
> *some or all of your current infrastructure.*

For example, contract labor outsourcing efforts are now choosing to configure third-party software to fit into the existing enterprise resource planning infrastructure, instead of bypassing the ERP altogether.

Therefore, adopt a Technology Integration Management (102) policy that advocates iterative infrastructure changes. During Proactive Project Oversight (97) assess the success of each integration point.

Pattern 109. Operational Data Transition

Today's e-business solutions rarely start with an empty database.[23] They acquire data elements from existing transactional systems and redefine them using XML.[24] This not only enables data standardization, it also makes up-to-the-minute data updates[25] possible.

> *Follow a methodology to define all e-business data using XML. Plan,*
> *schedule, and monitor the execution of how all data will actually be*
> *transferred from existing systems to the e-business.*

For example, contract labor outsourcing solutions often have a distinct subplan for data definition, validation, and transition. This plan usually includes supplier data and must satisfy tight system cutover timelines.

Therefore, create a subproject that methodically defines, acquires, and loads all needed data. Use Reusable Procedures Written in XML, Java, or SQL (83) to implement all data and all data access functions.

Pattern 110. Project Communications

Due to their scope and many stakeholders,[37] e-projects can fail or do poorly without excellent communications.[30,31] This requires a communication strategy and plan,[32] a project manager who is a good politician,[33] and tracking to ensure message congruence across organizations.[34]

> *Create a distinct subplan to define each project communication and when each communication will be delivered. Track it daily.*

For example, contract labor outsourcing efforts have roughly two dozen predefined communications (e.g., outsourcing award, project kickoff, supplier informational meeting announcement). Their delivery is defined in a subplan that is owned by a senior manager and is tracked daily.

Therefore, create a separate subplan for developing and delivering all Project Communications (110). Deliver all communications on time, and make sure each is received and understood as intended.

Pattern 111. End User Training

An e-business solution, like all software, requires end user training.[26] Experience shows that having and following through on a strategy and plan will yield good results.[27] Whether training is face to face or done online,[28] making it personally relevant is crucial to learning.[29,35]

> *Dedicate resources to develop, maintain, and execute a training strategy and plan. Design the training to be personally relevant.*

For example, training for a contract labor outsourcing solution is usually specialized for each major audience: managers, suppliers, contractor, and the program office. Training also very often receives its own subplan that includes strategy, coverage, schedule, and logistical needs.

Therefore, create a separate subplan for developing and delivering all End User Training (111). Make sure training is relevant to each distinct user group. Deliver all training on time, regardless of circumstances.

IMPLICATIONS OF PATTERN USE

When an Adaptable e-Business Connection (46) has a wide scope and is either technically, socially, or politically complex, its e-project must conduct Business Relationship

Management (103) to control its interconstrained subprojects, which must all execute in parallel. In particular:

- Program Office Formulation (105) should occur before Commodity Pricing (104) so that the program office can learn about the commodity, its pricing, and its fulfillment, before it assumes operational responsibility.
- Value Chain Transition (106) and Operational Data Transition (109) are often tightly intertwined because suppliers are sometimes the authoritative source of particular transactional data that must be loaded into the new solution.
- To minimize rework, Business Process Reengineering (107) must occur before Technology Configuration and Integration (108). Project Communications (110) must be carefully designed, planned, and executed, especially those that pertain to End User Training (111).

REFERENCES

1. Rayport, J. and Jaworski, B. (2003). *Introduction to e-Commerce.* McGraw-Hill.
2. Head, C. (2001). *Beyond Corporate Transformation.* Productivity Press.
3. Selig, G. (2003). Strategic Enterprise Initiatives—From Strategy to Implementation for Executives. In *Project World Seminar,* Boston, MA, June 2003.
4. Chu, C. and Smithson, S. Organizational Structure and e-Business: A Structural Analysis. In *Proceedings of the 5th International Conference on Electronic Commerce,* September 2003.
5. Rust, R. and Kannan, P. (2003). E-Service: A New Paradigm for Business in the Electronic Environment. *Communications of the ACM, 46,* 6, June.
6. Plant, R. (2003). *e-Commerce Formulation of Strategy.* Safari Tech Books Online, Inc.
7. He, N. and Milosevic, Z. (2001). B2B Contract Implementation Using Windows DNS. *Australian Computer Science Communications, 23,* 6, January.
8. Hammer, M. (2001). *The Agenda: What Every Business Must Do to Dominate the Decade.* Crown.
9. Reddington, T. and Chadbourne, B. (2004). Developing a Project Management Office. Presented at Boston University Corporate Seminar, MDP/118, June 2004.
10. Foti, R. (2003). Destination: Competitive Advantage. *PM Network, 17,* 8, August.
11. Damelio, R. (2001). *The Basics of Benchmarking.* Productivity Press.
12. Duvall, M. and Nash, K. (2004). A Shot at the Crown. *Baseline,* Issue 027, February.
13. Adshead, A. (2003). Web EDI Forces Suppliers to Change Tactics. *Computer Weekly,* July 1.
14. Whitehead Mann Group. (2002). The I-builders. *The Economist,* March 7, 2002.
15. Chung, A. (2003). By the Numbers: e-Sourcing Savings Start to Slow Down. *Baseline,* Issue 018, May.
16. Tapping, D. and Fabrizio, T. (2004). Value Stream Management: Eight Steps to Planning, Mapping and Sustaining Lean Improvements. *Productivity Press.*
17. Walsh, M., Cunnif, J., and Marino, D. (2004). Principles of Supply chain management. Presented at Boston University Corporate Seminar, MDP/213, May 2004.
18. Northey, P. and Southway, N. (2003). *Cycle Time Management.* Productivity Press.
19. Edelson, N. and Bennett, C. (2002). *Process Discipline.* Productivity Press.
20. Helle, P. and Marino, D. (2004). Business Process Analysis. Presented at Boston University Corporate Seminar, MDP/210, June 2004.

21. Hammer, M. (2001). The Superefficient Company. *Harvard Business Review,* September.

22. Bianchi, A., Caivano, D., and Vissaggio, G. (2003). Iterative Reengineering of Legacy Systems. *IEEE Transactions on Software Engineering, 29,* 3, March.

23. Czerniawska, F. and Potter, G. (2001). *Business in a Virtual World.* Ichor Business Books, Purdue University Press.

24. Hayashi, K. and Mizoguchi, R. (2003). Document Exchange Model for Augmenting Added Value of B2B Collaboration. In *Proceedings of the 5th International Conference on Electronic Commerce,* September 2003.

25. Burner, M. (2003). The Deliberate Revolution: Creating Connectedness with XML Web Services. *ACM Queue, 1,* 1, March.

26. Simonsen, M. and Sein, M. (2004). User Involvement in System Implementation. In *Proceedings of the Conference on Computer Personnel Research,* April 2004.

27. Grimes-Farrow, D. (1983). Human Factors Training and Awareness. In *Proceedings of the Annual Conference on Computers,* January 1983.

28. O'Brien, E. and Hall, T. (2004). Engineering E-Learning Systems (ELS): Training Needs Analysis. In *Proceedings of the ACM Symposium on Applied Computing,* March 2004.

29. Olfman, L. and Bostrom, R. (1988). The Influence of Training on Use of End-User Software. *ACM SIGOIS Bulletin, 9,* 2–3, April.

30. Atkins, S. and Gilbert, G. (2003). The Role of Induction and Training in Team Effectivness. *Project Management Journal, 34,* 2, June.

31. Finley, M. (2003). Communicate or Fail. *PM Network, 17,* 11, November.

32. Kayed, O. (2003). Seven Steps to Dynamic Scope Design. *PM Network, 17,* 12, December.

33. Anderson, A. (2003). Project Manager = Politician. In *Project World Seminar,* Boston, MA, June 2003.

34. Light, J. (1998). Keys to Successful Communication. *Journal of Management Consulting, 10,* 1, May.

35. Gordon, S. (1994). Systematic Training Program Design: Maximizing Effectiveness and Minimizing Liability. Prentice-Hall.

36. Spendolini, M. (1992). *The Benchmarking Book.* American Management Association.

37. Oschadleus, J. (2004). Communicate to Influence: Managing Project Stakeholders and Team Members. Presented at PMI Seminar, Orlando, FL, June, 2004.

38. Krovi, R., Chandra, A., and Rajagopalan, B. (2003). Information Flow Parameters for Managing Organizational Processes. *Communications of the ACM, 46,* 2, February.

39. Rust, R. and Kannan, P. (2003). E-Service: A New Paradigm for Business in the Electronic Environment. *Communications of the ACM, 46,* 6, June.

16

TEAM MANAGEMENT

Due its scope, complexity,[48] and number of stakeholders,[47] an e-project must take care to manage its relationships.[1,56] These relationships span the sponsoring organization,[2] the larger company,[3] the value chain,[4] and the user community.[5] Therefore, the project team should employ a multiteam management approach[49,51] and framework that enables customer focus, continuous improvement, total participation,[52] and societal networking.[6,52] There should also be subteams, each one capable of managing the relationship between the e-project and a specific constituency. The patterns involved are:

112. Project Team Framework
113. Steering Committee
114. Business Relationship Team
115. Program Office Team
116. Value Chain Team
117. Front Office Team
118. Back Office Team

The resulting team management framework would conceptually look like the one in Figure 16. Each distinct element, complex in its own right, has its own subteam. The Steering Committee (113) provides senior e-project oversight, and is also the final decision-making authority.

HOW TO INTERPRET FRAMEWORK #16

Due to its complexity and scope, an e-project should create a project team comprising distinct subteams, each with their own specialists. For contract labor management solutions, these sub-teams are as follows.

The Steering Committee (113) is made up of key project sponsors and stakeholders who have decision-making authority. The Business Relationship Team (114) comprises executives and lawyers who formally define the function, speed, quality, and cost of the

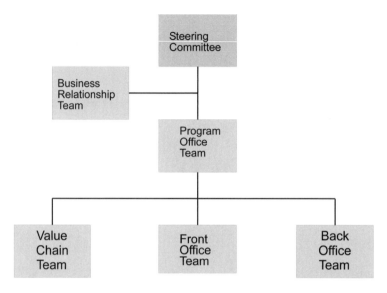

Figure 16. Framework #16: An e-project team comprises several subteams.

e-business connection. If the process is outsourced, a Program Office Team (115) is created to fill the managed service provider role. The Value Chain Team (116) is responsible for interviewing, qualifying, and signing on those suppliers that will satisfy the requirements of the e-business connection. The Front Office Team (117) comprises experts in order fulfillment, and the Back Office Team (118) comprises operational experts who ensure that the solution correctly operates across the entire Value Chain (25).

The remainder of this chapter details each of the patterns that, together, create Framework #16.

Pattern 112. Project Team Framework

An e-project often has several distinguishing attributes: distributed membership,[7] collaboration across geography,[8] strategic intent,[9] skill and cultural diversity,[10] organizational learning,[11,45,55] and dispute resolution.[12] Therefore, an e-project team requires a framework that supports cohesion, collaboration, geography, and stakeholders.[13,14,47]

> *Create a project teaming framework for collaboration, coordination, and learning among a number of highly specialized subteams.*

For example, contract labor outsourcing projects are too complicated for a single team. High degrees of specialization are needed for each major project area. Subteams are the only viable e-project team approach.

Therefore, design your Project Team Framework (112) first. Make sure it defines how the many highly specialized subteams will coordinate. Embed the subteam approach into the Solid Project Definition (92).

Pattern 113. Steering Committee

Despite the history of software project failure due to ineffective Steering committees,[15] many e-projects still operate without one. This subteam comprises sponsors and stake-holders[47] who select,[16] formulate,[17] and oversee[18] e-projects. When kept abreast of project status, it can become an effective change management[53,54] and issue resolution[46,50] body.

> *Create an effective steering committee comprising project sponsors and*
> *stakeholders to be responsible for oversight and issue resolution.*

For example, contract labor outsourcing impacts procurement, human resources, engineering, and manufacturing. Given their often diverse perspectives and areas of responsibility, a steering committee is often the only forum where these diverse groups can set common direction.

Therefore, create a Steering Committee (113) and charge it with formulating the e-project. Have the committee define the Project Constraints and Assumptions (91), and in doing so, establish an agreed-upon objective.

Pattern 114. Business Relationship Team

Knowing that Business Relationship Management (103) is the key to an e-business' success,[19] the second e-Project subteam to establish is the business relationship team. Their responsibility is the contractual definition (written, if at all possible, in XML[20]) of the e-business, including intent, strategy, speed, quality, and cost.[21,22]

> *Create a dedicated subteam to define and maintain the intent, strategy,*
> *speed, quality, and cost of the e-business relationship.*

For example, a business relation team for contract labor outsourcing is responsible for the request for proposal (RFP), the Master Service Agreement (18), and Flow Down (20) to supplier subcontracts.

Therefore, create a subteam that can define all formal e-business terms and conditions. Ensure the all members fully understand the Rapid "Go-to-Market" Strategy (7) and the intended Outsourced Process (16).

Pattern 115. Program Office Team

After e-project and e-business formulation, the program office[23] subteam is created to own the e-project policies and artifacts. Office staff are special people, in that they must think and work from multiple perspectives: strategic,[24] tactical,[24] service,[25,26] process,[27,28] and quality.[29]

> *Create a dedicated subteam to be responsible for the day-to-day business*
> *relationships that are implemented by the e-business.*

For example, contract labor outsourcing requires a dedicated team for day-to-day management of supplier contracts, supplier performance, resource planning, and the overall savings and performance goals as defined in the Master Agreement (18) for the Outsourced Process (16).

Therefore, create a Program Office to own Commodity Pricing (105), to own Process Change Management (101), to participate in Proactive Project Oversight (97), and to take over the Project Repository (96).

Pattern 116. Value Chain Team

Due to supply chain scope and complexity, each e-project needs a dedicated value chain subteam. It must comprise experts in supplier niches,[30] tiers,[31,32] variability,[33] qualification,[34,35] consolidation,[36,37] coordination,[25] and performance.[38] Members are either procured or come from the company that will own the Outsourced Process (16).

> *Create a dedicated subteam to identify, interview, qualify, and sign on*
> *those suppliers that will satisfy the e-business demand and perform*
> *satisfactorily under the e-business master agreement.*

For example, contract labor outsourcing projects can expend great effort to align all suppliers to the new rules of the Master Agreement (18). So a dedicated team is needed to own the Value Chain Transition (106).

Therefore, create a subteam that will define Flow Down (20) provisions from the Master Service Agreement (18) and bring the existing supplier community into alignment with those terms and conditions.

Pattern 117. Front Office Team

The front office team is the first service-oriented[26] subteam, created right after the Program Office Team (115). This team is responsible for the day-to-day service environment,[39] strategic and tactical operations,[24] Outsourced Process (16) help desk, and post-go-live End User Training (111).

> *Create a dedicated subteam to own and manage all day-to-day operations*
> *that will touch the entire end user population.*

For example, to attain a high percentage of correct transactions, a Front Office Team (117) for a contract labor outsourcing operation must act as a policy and procedure "help desk." In conjunction, all software interfaces point end users to the help desk (e.g., the splash page has its phone number).

Therefore, create a subteam that intimately understands all policies, procedures, and nuances of the Outsourced Process (16). Allow the end user community to have "7 by 24" access to this team. Assign each team member issue resolution responsibility for one specific end user group.

Pattern 118. Back Office Team

The back office subteam is created to develop an integration architecture[40] that defines invoicing and payment policies and procedures, integrates ERP systems, standardizes transactions,[41] simplifies integration complexity,[42] eliminates ad hoc and proprietary integrations,[43] and integrates offline and external data.[44]

> *Create a dedicated subteam to build a simple, standard, and nonproprietary B2B architecture that spans the value chain.*

For example, prior to process outsourcing, contractor data records are often on paper (e.g., invoices) and highly distributed (e.g., in supplier records), thus, consolidation and integration takes a big effort.

Therefore, create a subteam that will Inject Standards into Operations (9) across the entire e-business solution. Give this team Technology Integration Management (102) responsibility, which includes all data.

IMPLICATIONS OF PATTERN USE

When an Adaptable e-Business Connection (46) has a wide scope and is either technically, socially, or politically complex, the e-project must manage its relationships with all parties at all times. One successful approach is to create a Project Team Framework (112) to control the interconstrained subteams that must operate in parallel. Specifically:

- The Steering Committee (113) must be formed first so agreed-upon e-project goals and measures can be created. These decisions are crucial for the Business Relationship Team (114), which becomes responsible for contractually defining the Adaptable e-Business Connection (46). The Value Chain Team (116) should then be created so it can Flow Down (20) contractual provisions to Supplier Subtiers (24).
- The Program Office Team (115) must be formed right after the Master Agreement (18) so that it can help create the Front Office Team (117) and the Back Office Team (118). These subteams will take over operations under the management of the Program Office Team (115), right after deployment of the Adaptable e-Business Connection (46).

Yes, much time and attention must be given to the formation and maintenance of the e-project team. This is due to the nature of e-enterprise solutions—they are designed to operate in an event–response manner, with their processes spanning the entire company. Since companies are still mostly designed as distinct departments, a cross-department e-project team is required. With a well-designed team and committed management, the e-project initiative has the final pieces needed to give it the best chance for implementing an adaptable e-enterprise.

REFERENCES

1. Componation, P., Utley, D., and Swain, J. (2001). Using Risk Reduction to Measure Team Performance. *Engineering Management Journal, 13,* 4, December.
2. Little, J. and Hanna, E. (2003). Managing from the Inside Out. *Industrial Management, 45,* 6, November–December.

3. McDonough III, E. (2000). Meeting the Challenge of Global Team Management. *Research Technology Management, 43,* 4, July–August.

4. Brizz, M. (1998). The Ultimate Advantage: Forging Stronger Partnerships with Your Clients. *Journal of Management Consulting, 10,* 1, May.

5. Eveleth, D. and Baker-Eveleth, L. (2003). Developing Dialogue Skill. *Journal of Education for Business, 78,* 4, March–April.

6. Walden, D. and Shiba, S. (2002). *Four Practical Revolutions in Management.* Productivity Press.

7. Foti, R. (2003). Today's Project Manager. *PM Network, 17,* 4, April.

8. Foti, R. (2004). The Virtual Hand Shake. *PM Network, 18,* 3, March.

9. Cleland, D. and Ireland, L. (2004). *Project Management: Strategic Design and Implementation.* Project Management Institute Press.

10. Ladika, S. (2003). Treat Diversity as Your Asset for Uncommon Gains. *PM Network, 17,* 11, November.

11. Love, P., Irani, Z., and Edwards, D. (2003). Learning to Reduce Rework in Projects. *Project Management Journal, 34,* 3, September.

12. Ingebretsen, M. (2003). Taming the Beast. *PM Network, 17,* 7, July.

13. Mullaly, M. (2003). Co-operation, Collaboration and Conflict: Insights into Managing Great Teams. Presented at Project World Seminar, Boston, MA, June 2003.

14. Chan, S. (2000). E-commerce Workforce Development Strategies: A Dialogue with Industry. In *Proceedings of the 2000 ACM SIGCPR Conference on Computer Personnel Research,* April 2000.

15. Skeen, D. (1977). User Involvement with EDP Systems Development. In *Proceedings of the 15th Annual SIGCPR Conference,* August 1977.

16. McKeen, J. and Guimaraes, T. (1985). Selecting MIS Projects by Steering Committee. *Communications of the ACM, 28,* 12, December.

17. Brown, C. and Magill, S. (1992). Designing the IS organization: Aligning the Systems Development Function with the Business. In *Proceedings of the 1992 ACM SIGCPR Conference on Computer Personnel Research,* May 1992.

18. Doll, W. and Torkzadeh, G. (1987). The Relationship of MIS Steering Committees to Size of Firm and Formalization of MIS Planning. *Communications of the ACM, 30,* 11, November.

19. Chu, C. and Smithson, S. Organizational Structure and e-Business: A Structural Analysis. In *Proceedings of the 5th International Conference on Electronic Commerce,* September.

20. He, N. and Milosevic, Z. (2001). B2B Contract Implementation Using Windows DNS. *Australian Computer Science Communications, 23,* 6, January.

21. Nader, D., Gerstein, M., and Shaw, R. (2004). *Organizational Architecture: Designs for Changing Organizations.* Project Management Institute Press.

22. Suri, R. (2002). *Quick Response Manufacturing.* Productivity Press.

23. Kerzner, H. (2003). Strategic Planning for a Project Office. *Project Management Journal, 34,* 2, June.

24. Reddington, T. and Chadbourne, B. (2004). Developing a Project Management Office. Presented at Boston University Corporate Seminar, MDP/118, June 2004.

25. Gibbs, J., Kraemer, K., and Dedrick, J. (2003). Environment and Policy Factors Shaping Global E-Commerce Diffusion: A Cross-Country Comparison. *Information Society, 19,* 1, January.

26. Lim, B. and Wen, J. (2003). Web Services: An Analysis of the technology, Its benefits, and Implementation Difficulties. *Information Systems Management, 20,* 2, Spring.

27. Hammer, M. (2001). The Superefficient Company. *Harvard Business Review,* September.

28. Badir, Y., Founou, R., Stricker, C., and Bourquin, V. (2003). Management of Global Large-

Scale Projects through a Federation of Multiple Web-Based Workflow Management Systems. *Project Management Journal, 34,* 3, September.

29. Foti, R. (2003). Destination: Competitive Advantage. *PM Network, 17,* 8, August.

30. Stoffer, H. (2003). Supplier Group Touts Greener World. *Automotive News, 78,* 6057, August.

31. Adshead, A. (2003). Web EDI Forces Suppliers to Change Tactics. *Computer Weekly,* July 1.

32. Teltzrow, M., Günther, O., and Pohle, C. (2003). Analyzing Consumer Behavior at Retailers with Hybrid Distribution Channels: A Trust Perspective. In *Proceedings of the 5th International Conference on Electronic Commerce.* September 2003

33. Walsh, M., Cunnif, J., and Marino, D. (2004). Principles of Supply Chain management. Presented at Boston University Corporate Seminar, MDP/213, May 2004.

34. Chung, A. (2003). By the Numbers: e-Sourcing Savings Start to Slow Down. *Baseline,* Issue 018, May.

35. Houghton, T., Markham, B., and Tevelson, B. (2002). Performance Metrics—Design Performance with a Goal to Achieve Competitive Advantage, Thinking Strategically about Supply Management. *Supply Chain Management Review, 6,* 5, September.

36. Doran, D. and Roome, R. (2003). An Evaluation of Value-Transfer within a Modular Supply Chain. *Journal of Automobile Engineering, 217,* 7, July.

37. Tapping, D. and Fabrizio, T. (2004). *Value Stream Management: Eight Steps to Planning, Mapping and Sustaining Lean Improvements.* Productivity Press.

38. Nolan, S. (2003). Calculating Costs of Extending Real-Time Replenishment. *Baseline,* Issue 020, July.

39. Fuxman, A., Giorgini, P., Kolp, M., and Mylopoulos, J. (2001). Information Systems as Social Structures. In *Proceedings of the International Conference on Formal Ontology in Information Systems,* Volume 2001, October 2001.

40. Bussler, C. (2001). Semantic B2B Integration. In *Proceedings of the 2001 Proceedings of the 2001 ACM SIGMOD International Conference on the Management of Data,* Vol. 29, No. 2, May 2001.

41. Bussler, C. (2002). Data Management Issues in Electronic Commerce: The Role of B2B Engines in B2B Integration Architectures. *ACM SIGMOD Record, 31,* 1, March.

42. Chieu, T., Fu, S., Pinel, F., and Yih, J. (2003). Unified Solution for Procurement Integration and B2B Stores. In *Proceedings of the 5th International Conference on Electronic Commerce,* September 2003.

43. Dogac, A., Tambag, Y., Pembecioglu, P., Pektas, S., Laleci, G., Kurt, G., Toprak, S., and Kabak, Y. (2002). Beyond Relational Tables: An ebXML Infrastructure Implementation Through UDDI Registries and RosettaNet PIPs. In *Proceedings of the 2002 ACM SIGMOD International Conference on the Management of Data,* Vol. 30, No. 2, June 2002.

44. Nemati, H., Barko, C., and Moosa, A. (2003). E-CRM Analytics: The Role of Data Integration. *Journal of Electronic Commerce in Organizations, 1,* 3, July–September.

45. Cetindamar, D. (2004). Learning through E: Organizational Learning in Implementation. In *Proceedings of the 13th International Conference for the Management of Technology,* April 2004.

46. Phillips, D. (2003). *A Project Manager's Guide to Working with People on Projects.* IEEE Computer Society Press.

47. Oschadleus, J. (2004). Communicate to Influence: Managing Project Stakeholders and Team Members. Presented at PMI Seminar, Orlando, Florida, June, 2004.

48. Xia, W. and Lee, G. (2004). Grasping the Complexity of IS Development Projects. *Communications of the ACM, 47,* 5, May.

49. Chiang, R. and Mookerjee, V. (2004). Improving Software Team Productivity. *Communications of the ACM, 47,* 5, May.

50. Glaser, A., Fu, S., and Tumelty, M. (2004). Growing a Participatory Programming Environment. *Communications of the ACM, 47,* 6, June.

51. Gorla, N. and Lam, Y. (2004). Who Should Work with Whom? Building Effective Software Project Teams. *Communications of the ACM, 47,* 6, June.

52. Tiwana, A. (2003). Affinity to Infinity in Peer-to-Peer Knowledge Platforms. *Communications of the ACM, 46,* 5, May.

53. Vanhoenacker, J., Bryant, A., and Dedene, G. (1999). Creating a Knowledge Management Architecture for Business Process Change. In *Proceedings of the 1999 ACM SIGCPR Conference on Computer Personnel Research,* April 1999.

54. Sato, S. and Panton, A. (2003). Using a Change-Management Approach to Promote Customer-Centered Design. In *Proceedings of the 2003 Conference on Designing for User experiences,* June 2003.

55. Singh, M. (2004). *The Practical Handbook of Internet Computing.* Chapman & Hall/CRC Press.

56. Grief, I. (2004). The Socialization of Collaboration. *Computerworld,* August 25.

Appendix A

CASE STUDY BACKGROUND

The case study for this book comes from the staffing industry. Although little formal research exists about e-business, e-process, e-commerce, or e-project for staffing, this industry has a history of implementing many an Adaptable e-Business Connection (46). The reasons for this follow.

To improve overall control and cost of contract labor, many companies are migrating to a comprehensive solution that includes an Outsourced Process (16) that is supported by vendor management system (VMS) technology. Successful labor management outsourcing comes from an e-project that includes goals such as increased labor quality at reduced cost, standard processes, improved supplier performance, and anywhere, anytime transactions supported by Internet-based technology.

A personalized, Internet-enabled, contract labor management service can simultaneously respond to contract labor demand flux, adapt to business changes, and generate savings and efficiencies. While the Outsourced Process (16) is generating savings, business leaders concentrate on strategy, and suppliers both reduce their cost of doing business and optimize their operations to better meet needs. The following outline shows how this is accomplished

A.1. Business Drivers
- A.1.1. Cost and Compliance Issues
- A.1.2. Vendor Management Technology
- A.1.3. Potential Savings
- A.1.4. Process Outsourcing

A.2. Business Change
- A.2.1. Trusted Partnerships
- A.2.2. Performance Standards
- A.2.3. Standard Pricing
- A.2.4. Web-Enabled Transactions

A.3. Open Process Solution
- A.3.1. Outsourced Managed Services
- A.3.2. Centralized Process Knowledge
- A.3.3. Optimal Pricing
- A.3.4. Fully Integrated Infrastructure

A.1. BUSINESS DRIVERS

One crucial discussion among today's business leaders concerns contract labor management and its cost. To improve overall control and cost of contract labor, many companies are seeking a comprehensive solution having an Outsourced Process (16) supported by vendor management system (VMS) technology. The VMS is the one solution component that is currently being most heavily evaluated and scrutinized prior to implementation. Implementation of the overall solution typically occurs in three stages: (a) reduce commodity cost, create process efficiencies, and enforce supplier compliance; (b) optimize and compress the supply chain; and (c) add services that yield high value.

So, many companies are now seeking advice on how to best create an enterprise-wide e-business solution that maximizes overall cost savings. Experience indicates that cost savings and operational efficiencies are optimal with a solution consisting of an Outsourced Process (16) supported by a VMS that is either a component of, or directly integrates with, the existing enterprise resource planning (ERP) system or its functional equivalent. When correctly designed, it is common for this solution to generate roughly 15% in overall labor savings while also gaining 15% in cost avoidance.

A.1.1. Cost and Compliance Issues

One of the most urgent discussions among today's business leaders is contract labor management, its total cost of ownership, and its commodity-level costs.[1] However, contract labor is not simply a resource issue. Globalization, outsourcing, competitive pressures, acquisitions, mergers, and a less safe international environment all contribute to reshaping domestic and global contract labor management. Those in procurement, human resources, and senior management are faced with the challenge of providing high-quality support programs while also trying to lower costs and developing a large contingent of "specialists" and "globalists."

Efforts to date have focused on policies and strategies designed to achieve efficient contract labor management. Issues such as a diverse employee population, rapid movement into new locations, managing and consolidating vendors, and containing costs are being addressed. These forces tend to drive implementations into the three aforementioned stages: (a) reduce cost, create efficiencies, and improve compliance; (b) compress the supply chain; and (c) add high-value services.

A.1.2. Vendor Management Technology

One technology that is now being seriously considered is the vendor management system[2] (VMS). This technology, typically built upon Internet tools such as Ariba[20] and Commerce One,[3] has recently emerged as a solution for managing contract labor transactions (e.g., requisitions, submittals, time cards, and invoices). Currently, potential buyers of VMS technology are evaluating whether or not VMS will help them meet all their goals of contingent contract labor rebuilding and cost management. Central to their evaluation is whether to keep their labor management process and acquire the technology, or outsource their contract labor management process to a highly experienced firm that also has a VMS technology.

A.1.3. Potential Savings

Many companies are also seeking advice on creating a business solution that maximizes overall cost savings.[4] The driving consideration is to reduce the "hard" labor cost. However, some executives strongly feel that "soft" costs, such as manager and accounting staff time, mount up fast when the contract labor management process is poorly defined or not enforced. Therefore, efficiency is often a strong secondary consideration, and achieving it by outsourcing is a common approach.

A well-designed outsourced process (i.e., not just a VMS purchase) can create a highly controlled, open, and competitive environment. When designed and implemented well, such a solution can achieve roughly 15% in labor savings while gaining back 15% in staff time. To achieve these gains, companies are seeking council from industry pundits and staffing firms who are known to be experts in this area.

A.1.4. Process Outsourcing

Experience indicates that cost savings and operational efficiencies are maximized by a comprehensive solution comprising an Outsourced Process (16) supported by a VMS technology. This solution is, therefore, a functional outsource. An outsourced contract labor management process supported by a VMS is one kind of e-business solution. Current reports from the field indicate that companies successful with e-business initiatives assign senior executives to the projects.[5] They then oversee a project in the following way.

They first get the business rules in place for integrating suppliers and for building on existing supplier strengths, and then they address technical considerations. Essential e-project elements are project governance, approval board, dedicated e-business team, and implementation plan. Key project deliverables are "to-be" processes, organizational impact analysis, return on investment, performance metrics, and a VMS technology evaluation[6] (e.g., scalability, flexibility, viability, etc.). Such a project positions a company to outsource the desired process to a third-party company. The outsourced process, which can be implemented at no direct cost to the company, shifts "soft" costs to the service provider. The VMS supports the new process and helps enforce "hard" savings.

A.2. BUSINESS CHANGE

Successful outsourcing comes from a project that has goals such as increased labor quality at reduced cost, standard process, improved supplier performance, and anywhere, anytime transactions supported by Internet-based technology. These projects, when successful, concentrate on achieving four key goals: one for the business, one for the process outsourcing, one for procurement, and one for operations.

A key business goal is to leverage existing supplier relationships through "trusted" partnerships while reducing contract administration cost and risk. A key outsource goal is to use the opportunity to "shore up" suppliers to new performance standards. A key procurement goal is to help buyers easily interact with many suppliers to increase contract labor quality while reducing labor cost through leveraged pricing. A key operational goal is to reduce workload through Web-enabled anywhere, anytime transactions (e.g., orders, submittals, time cards, and invoices).

Experience with this approach overwhelmingly points to one strategy—companies successful with implementing enterprise-wide contract labor management solutions create a formal project to accomplish the above goals on the first try. These companies do not underestimate the complexity and scope of the effort, even though many people expect e-business initiatives to be "quick" solutions. Some of today's staffing companies have over 15 years of experience in helping their customers formulate and conduct formal projects for contract labor management.

A.2.1. Trusted Partnerships

A key business goal is to leverage existing supplier relationships through "trusted" partnerships[7] while reducing contract labor management administration cost and risk. Successful e-projects have an explicit goal to cultivate and maintain the trust of all project stakeholders. In fact, trust issues are often the number one priority for companies seeking new partners.[7] For contract labor management, incumbent supplier trust is crucial to maintaining timely labor acquisition. The Outsourced Process (16) establishes a point of control for leveraging the supplier base, but that does not mean existing suppliers are valued any less. In fact, those who agree to follow the new process enjoy steady orders without having to sell. This agreement comes in the form of a "subcontract" that defines the rules of engagement. The owner of the Outsourced Process (16) thus assumes the risk of the appropriate Flow Down (20), execution, and enforcement of contractual provisions to all Supplier Subtiers (24).

A.2.2. Performance Standards

A key outsource goal is to use the opportunity to "shore up" suppliers to new performance standards. When completed, an outsourcing project puts one staffing firm in the position of being the full-service provider.[8] Part of that company's job is to establish a Program Office Team (115) for explaining the new contract labor management program and for managing suppliers according to program standards. Some typical standards are expected order fulfillment times, price standards for particular labor skill sets, adherence to temporary assignment duration policies, and proper fit of candidate skills to those skills defined in the order. Thus, the project is a key opportunity to align the supplier base to the desired process.

A.2.3. Standard Pricing

A key procurement goal is to help buyers interact with many suppliers to increase contract labor quality while reducing labor cost through leveraged pricing. A flexible technology for interconnecting buyers and suppliers of contract labor is an "extranet"—a secure, private Internet connection between the parties. VMS technology can create an extranet for each outsourced contract labor management program. Buyers use the VMS to create their orders. The Program Office Team (115) ensures that orders meet the pricing standards and are distributed to all the right suppliers. Suppliers use the VMS to submit candidates for each order, and the program office team ensures that only the best candidates are presented. The combination of program office team and VMS technology leverages a buyer's ability to interact with suppliers who have already been qualified to respond with the best candidate for the least cost. That cost is reduced due to the combined volume of all orders. This "volume pricing" occurs when guaranteed orders are targeted to Supplier Subtiers (24), thus causing a reduction in overall fulfillment cost.

A.2.4. Web-Enabled Transactions

A key operational goal is to reduce workload through Web-enabled transactions (e.g., orders, submittals, time cards, and invoices). Internet technology can transform a company because it integrates e-business capabilities into every aspect of value creation, such as procurement. Internet technology can enable a company to extend its reach[10] because it spans geography and time zones. This is especially germane for contract labor management. Some firms use VMS technology as a tool for reaching those remote sites where it has been difficult to enforce price standards that yield savings. Others use VMS technology to significantly reduce manager workload (e.g., screening a great number of resumes and approving time cards and expense reports, especially from people working in remote locations or working abroad in countries where the company has no offices). Such cost avoidance can be significant—often 6 hours per week per hiring manager. Similar "cost avoidance" is achieved on the administrative side.

A.3. OPEN PROCESS SOLUTION

A personalized, Internet-enabled, contract labor management service can simultaneously respond to contract labor demand flux, adapt to business change, and generate savings and efficiencies. A dedicated on-site team of staffing experts, called the Program Office Team (115), provides a highly personalized contract labor management service. The Program Office Team (115) is designed to understand a particular business and to rapidly respond to peaks in labor demand brought about by the natural cycles of the business. The standard pricing schedule (i.e., rate card), often embedded in the VMS technology, becomes part of the Common Body of Knowledge (13) and expectation. The program office team is responsible for enforcing the pricing, thereby eliminating "rogue" supplier activity and "special deals" that increase costs. Underneath it all is a scalable digital infrastructure, comprising a VMS "front office" and an ERP "back office" infrastructure.

A.3.1. Outsourced Managed Services

A dedicated onsite team of staffing experts, the Program Office Team (115), provides highly personalized contract labor management service. Typical providers of contract labor outsourcing solutions use a service-oriented approach. They first compile a team of staffing experts into a program office team. These people understand the complexities and dynamics of enterprise-wide contract labor management. They focus on hiring temporary labor based on tactical concerns[4] (e.g., "hot skills" fulfillment, labor mobilization/demobilization, current labor value, core competency retention, and resource planning). The program office manager typically works with business leaders on strategic concerns[4] (e.g., resource planning, labor usage policy, permanent-to-temporary ratio, skill set mix, pricing schedule analysis, and supplier performance).

A.3.2. Centralized Process Knowledge

The Program Office Team (115) is designed to understand the particular business nuances of the outsourcing firm and to rapidly respond to peaks in labor demand brought about by the natural cycles of that business. The program office team is typically staffed with dedicated skill set and fulfillment experts who understand their customer's particular business and industry. These professionals pay attention to the business cycles (e.g., healthcare open enrollment periods, seasonal power plant outages). Backing up the program office team is often a national network of offices, often in close proximity to each key business location. The program office team is also often part of a dedicated service delivery organization with executive ownership. The breadth, depth. and personalization of this service are unique to supply chain solutions.[11]

A.3.3. Optimal Pricing

The standard pricing schedule (i.e., the rate card), often embedded in the VMS,[12] quickly becomes part of common knowledge and expectation. Cost management, a key task in the service-oriented approach, is based on a pricing schedule, sometimes called a rate card. Once created, the pricing schedule is often embedded in the VMS technology, so it automatically appears when a person creates an order. To create optimal pricing, the program office team taps its broad knowledge of current market conditions and labor prices across the geography spanned by the customer's business. That knowledge, historical contract labor trends, and geography-specific wage and salary benchmarks are gathered, analyzed, and compared. The result is pricing that will attract quality talent and deliver optimal savings.

A.3.4. Fully Integrated Infrastructure

Underneath it all is a scalable digital infrastructure, comprising a VMS "front office," an ERP "back office," and integration architecture. The solution just described is, in effect, a complex Value Chain (25). Prior to the process outsourcing, the value chain might have comprised multiple, often localized, trading partnerships. After the process outsourcing, the Program Office Team (115) becomes the control point for eliminating supply chain fragmentation and for transforming the buying process. This creates an environment for savings and efficiencies. But all this would not be possible without the implementation of a scalable digital infrastructure[13] designed to integrate with all business entities. Concurrent with program office team implementation, the VMS is configured to become the e-business portal through which the business and the labor supply chain transact. The VMS also connects to the ERP, which thus creates a seamless, end-to-end technical platform. Current trends suggest that within the not too distant future, the end-to-end technology platform will reside in a single hosting environment.[20]

A.4. BUSINESS BENEFITS

While the Outsourced Process (16) is generating savings, business leaders concentrate on strategy, and suppliers reduce their cost of doing business and optimize their operations to better meet customer needs. The outsourced process generates overall savings without requiring managers to concern themselves with trying to control supplier profits. Thus, the solution handles the "tactical" aspects. It improves reporting and reduces workload and risk, thus freeing up business leaders to concentrate on the "strategic" aspects. During the transition to the new solution, suppliers are formally qualified to meet expected contract labor needs. Qualified suppliers are able to (a) reduce their cost of doing business, (b) focus their resources on satisfying particular contract labor needs, and (c) involve formerly non-participating offices as new customer needs arise. Through one URL, suppliers obtain a "24-7 ability" to transact, respond, and understand their performance against program metrics. Thus, the solution not only generates savings, it generates durability as well.

A.4.1. Commodity and Process Savings

The Outsourced Process (16) generates overall savings without requiring managers to concern themselves with trying to control supplier profits.[14] Definitions of "value" are often expressed as a ratio of benefits received versus their cost. A comprehensive contract labor outsourcing solution goes beyond this simple get-and-give ratio. The solution not only delivers value by constraining price, it is designed to free up the outsourcing organization. The powerful combination of solid program management enabled by VMS technology creates numerous operational efficiencies.[12] The net result is often 15% less overall effort for "transactional touches" by every person involved with managing or administering some aspect of the contract labor. That equates to almost one day per week per person.

A.4.2. Tool for Strategic Planning

The highly adaptable solution handles the tactical aspects. It improves reporting and reduces workload and risk, thus freeing up business leaders to concentrate on the strategic aspects. Outsourcing creates a single access point for the entire process and all downstream (e.g., orders) and upstream (e.g., submittals) flows.[11] The VMS is the transaction tool, so data for monitoring, tracking, and reporting activity reside in one database. This lets the Program Office Team (115) manage the process, thus reducing manager workload and liability (e.g., coemployment, minority/diversity target noncompliance). The reporting allows the human resources department to increase its ability to contribute to strategic planning,[15] and to extend its reach[10] to locations that heretofore could not be controlled because of distance. With the tactical aspects under control, business leaders can concentrate on strategic concerns such as competition,[16] global sourcing,[11] business expansion,[10] or accelerating an acquisition, merger, or alliance,[11] all the while knowing that the whole solution will work.

A.4.3. No Supplier Selling

At the same time, suppliers are able to reduce their cost of doing business, focus their resources on satisfying particular contract labor needs, and quickly involve their other offices as new customer needs arise. The transition to an outsourced process creates several opportunities for suppliers. First, a sales force is not needed to generate orders. This translates into a direct cost reduction and into efficiency, because sales may not always generate orders targeted to the supplier's niche.[14] Second, small niche suppliers and minority/women-owned suppliers can now, due the Internet portal, be as responsive as larger, more dominant, suppliers[17] who can afford to dedicate a sales force.[10] Third, efficiency occurs because suppliers have to learn and use only one workflow, instead of having to learn and use different procedures for each department within a company.[18] The fourth opportunity is the very low cost for suppliers (i.e., a browser and minimal training) to enable more of its offices to participate in the contract labor program.[19]

A.4.4. Monitored Performance

Through one URL, suppliers obtain a "7 by 24" ability to transact, respond, and understand their required performance against program metrics.[10] The Internet is on all the time, so suppliers are better able to audit (e.g., time card hours) and approve (e.g., expense report) transactions. Regarding performance, the e-project clearly defines, documents, and communicates supplier performance metrics before the new process goes live. Typical metrics define speed (e.g., fill time), quality (e.g., number of on-time starts), and cost (e.g., average bill rate). The VMS captures these metrics, as appropriate, for each transaction. Through their Internet portal, suppliers are given "7 by 24" access to all usage reports, including their performance against the metrics. This allows suppliers to be diligent about their participation in the contract labor outsourcing program, and to quickly adjust their operations if they find they are not meeting standards.

REFERENCES

1. LoPorto, J., Dalessio, J., and Paschall C. (2004). New Trends and Responses to Global Mobility. Presented at New England Human Resource Association Panel Discussion, Newton Marriott Hotel, March 26, 2004.

2. Staffing Industry Analysts, Inc. (2003). VMS Decision 2003 Conference. http://www.staffingindustry.com/, October 2003.

3. Commerce One, Inc. (2004). Commerce One Market Side Portal Solution 3.0. http://www.commerceone.com/, January 2004.

4. Staffing Industry Analysts, Inc. (2004). Contingent Contract Labor Strategies Publication. http://www.staffingindustry.com/publications/cws.html, March 2004.

5. Eduard, T. (2001). Adding Clicks to Bricks. *Consulting to Management—C2M, 12,* 4, December.

6. Rifkin, G. and & Kurtzman, J. (2002). Is Your e-Business Plan Radical Enough? *MIT Sloan Management Review, 43,* 3, March.

7. Sultan, F. and Mooraj, H. (2001). Design a Trust-based e-Business Strategy. *Marketing Management, 10,* 4, November–December.

8. Weill, P. and Vitale, M. (2001). *Place to Space: Migrating to e-Business Models.* Harvard Business School Press.

9. Ling, R. and Yen, D. (2001). Extranet: A New Wave of Internet. *S.A.M. Advanced Management Journal, 66,* 2, February.

10. Cavusgil, S. (2002). Extending the Reach of e-Business. *Marketing Management, 11,* 2, March–April.

11. Mentzer, J., DeWitt, W., Keebler, J., and Min, S. (2001). Defining Supply Chain Management. *Journal of Business Logistics, 22,* 2, February.

12. Tobias, H. (2002). Using e-Business to Gain Advantage. *Journal of Database Marketing, 9,* 2, February.

13. Ribbers, P. and Schoo, K. (2002). Program Management and Complexity of ERP Implementations. *Engineering Management Journal, 14,* 2, June.

14. Smith, G. E. (2002). Segmenting B2B Markets with Economic Value Analysis. *Marketing Management, 11,* 2, March–April.

15. Targowski, A. and Deshpande, S. (2001). The Utility and Selection of an HRIS. *Advances in Competitiveness Research, 9,* 1, January.

16. Cohan, P. (2002). E-commerce Equals Empowerment. *Financial Executive, 18,* 3, March.

17. Staffing Industry Analysts, Inc. (2003). Largest Staffing Companies Continue to Dominate Industry. http://www.staffingindustry.com/news_releases/20030825.html, August 2003.

18. Alonso, J. (2002). CRM the "Ecosystem" Difference. *Pharmaceutical Executive, 22,* 8, August.

19. Schultz, B. (2002). Assembling a Top-of-the-Line Web Services Model. *Network World, 19,* 7, July.

20. Chieu, T., Fu, S., Pinel, F., and Yih, J. (2003). Unified Solution for Procurement Integration and B2B Stores. In *Proceedings of the 5th International Conference on Electronic Commerce,* September 2003.

OPEN PROCESS EXAMPLE

The Internet-based process component of the solution for the case study (see Appendix A) is summarized in this appendix. It is an excerpt from the total open process solution that was generated by the OpenProcess™ software product. This software product was developed by OpenProcess, Inc.

The total open process solution comprises 166 Web pages, 41 glossary terms, 43 supporting documents, and 18 e-forms. It has hyperlinks to roughly 500 contractually required reports that are automatically generated by the solution's Web-based software application.

The larger solution comprises a Web-based software application that supports all transactions and two accounting systems built on ERP technology. This solution has been in operation for over seven years. The open process portion of that solution was taken out of service roughly four years ago, after it was re-implemented into a VMS product that now supports the entire contract labor management program.

This solution is typical in size and complexity for an average outsourced contract labor management process. The process component alone is far too large to fit within this book. Therefore, this appendix summarizes how the process is organized and viewed, and also provides real examples of process Web pages, glossary terms, supporting documents, e-forms, and reports. These examples are organized as follows:

Structure and Appearance
    B.1.   Process Organization and Conventions
    B.2.   The Human–Computer Interface
    B.3.   The Navigation Frame
    B.4.   The Work Area Frame
    B.5.   The Keyword Frame
Process Web Pages
    B.6.   Managed Staffing Program (A0)
    B.7.   Program Management (A1)
    B.8.   Customer Relations and Opportunities (A11)

Links to Live Data

B.1. PROCESS ORGANIZATION AND CONVENTIONS

Typically, processes contain hundreds, sometimes thousands, of distinct work activities. Such a number is far too large for any one person to comprehend, remember, or use. Therefore, people have invented ways to organize all the detailed work activities for a process into one complete and coherent collection. The OpenProcess™ product uses the process organization standard of the United States Air Force, called IDEF0.

IDEF0 organizes all the detailed work activities for a process into a single hierarchy, often called a "tree structure." The root of the tree (i.e., the top of the process) is labeled "A0." (The letter "A" is an abbreviation for "activity.") This is the highest-level process description. The IDEF0 method "breaks down" the A0 into several more detailed descriptions. Each description is a distinct part of the A0, and when taken together, they completely detail it. Descriptions at this level are labeled "A1" to "A9." Similarly, these descriptions are broken down into more detailed descriptions (e.g., the A1 description is broken into "A11" through "A19").

Figure B-1 is a graphic excerpt from the IDEF0 organization of the Internet-based process for the case study. This chart shows the A0 level, the A1 through A9 level, and the level that details the A1. The shaded boxes are those activities that are discussed later in this section.

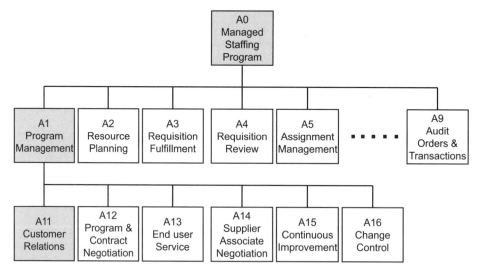

Figure B.1. A graphic depiction of process organization.

B.2. THE HUMAN–COMPUTER INTERFACE

Many years of experience with Internet-based processes had led me to design a particular human–computer interface having three distinct parts:

1. **Navigation Frame.** A thin space that allows a person to quickly navigate the process.
2. **Work Area Frame.** A large space that has two purposes. First, to allow a person to read and follow process steps. Second, to allow a person to read glossary terms or documents, use e-forms and software applications, and read reports.
3. **Keyword Frame.** A thin space that contains a book-like index of all process key-words. Each keyword is a hyperlink to a glossary term, document, e-form, software application, or report.

The three frames are place on the computer screen, left to right or right to left, the orientation corresponding to the direction people read their written language (e.g., English is read left to right, whereas Arabic is read right to left). The work area frame is always placed in the middle, and the navigation frame and keyword frame have "hide" buttons to enable the user to dynamically maximize the width of the work area frame. Figure B.2 conceptually depicts this interface.

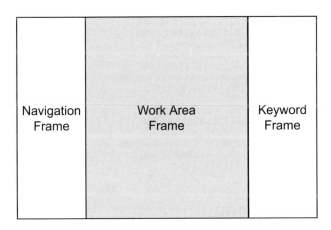

Figure B.2. A human–computer interface for a Web-based process.

B.3. THE NAVIGATION FRAME

The navigation frame contains the process menu. Since the process organization is a hierarchy, the menu is an indented outline. Buttons on the left enable outline expansion and contraction. Each line in the menu is a hyperlink to an actual process Web page. A sample menu is shown in Figure B.3.

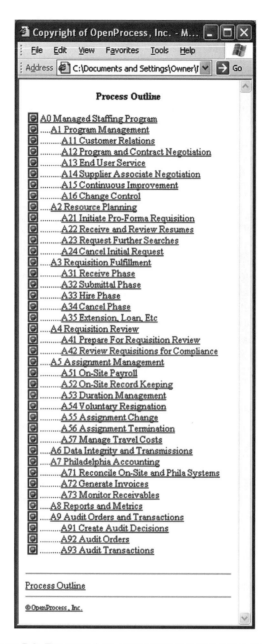

Figure B.3. The menu for a contract labor management process.

B.4. THE WORK AREA FRAME

The work area frame presents process descriptions. It is also the area in which glossary terms, documents, e-forms, software application GUIs, and reports are displayed when the user clicks on a hyperlink in the keyword frame. Figure B.4 shows a sample work area containing a process step.

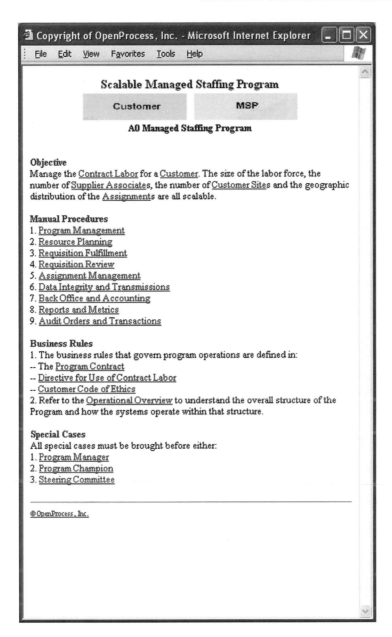

Figure B.4. A process work area for contract labor management.

B.5. THE KEYWORD FRAME

The keyword frame contains a glossary of the keywords for the process. A very effective form of organization is a book-like index (i.e., a "keyword in context" list). Each keyword is a hyperlink to a glossary term, document, e-form, software application, or report. A partial keyword list is shown in Figure B.5.

Figure B.5. Partial keyword list for contract labor management.

B.6. MANAGED STAFFING PROGRAM (A0)

When users first logs into the Internet-based process, they are brought to the highest-level process description, the A0 level (i.e., the top). Good descriptions will give the process objective, list the major process areas, list the major business rules, and identify all special cases, as shown in Figure B.6.

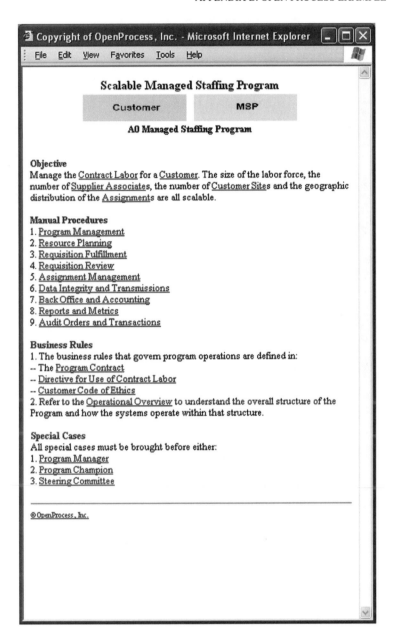

Figure B.6. Top process description for contract labor management.

B.7. PROGRAM MANAGEMENT (A1)

As shown in Figure B.6, the A0 process description lists between one and nine major process areas. Each one of these major areas has a description that is of the same format as the A0 process. This helps users quickly get accustomed to reading process descriptions (Figure B.7).

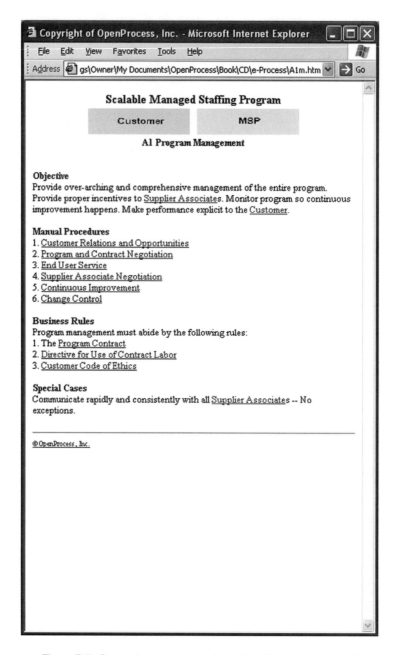

Figure B.7. One major process area for contract labor management.

B.8. CUSTOMER RELATIONS AND OPPORTUNITIES (A11)

Typically, each major process area (i.e., the "Ax" level) comprises one to nine detailed process descriptions. You know that you are at the lowest level of detail in a process when the process description becomes a narrative and not a list of process steps (Figure B.8).

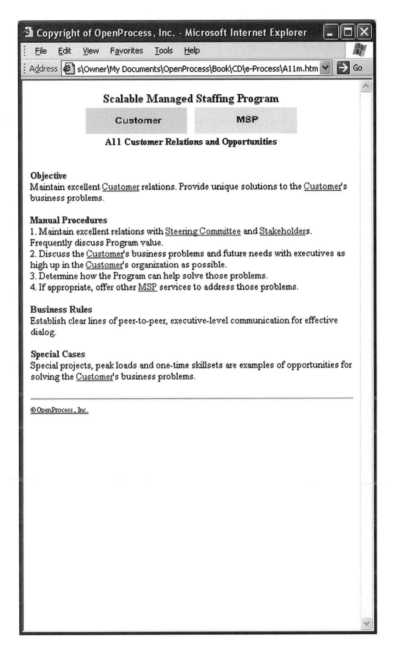

Figure B.8. A detailed process description within contract labor management.

B.9. KEYWORD HYPERLINK TO GLOSSARY TERM

Processes have underlying terminologies. Every process has roughly a few dozen absolutely essential terms (e.g., "supplier associate" for this case study). Thus, each critical term gets its own hyperlink at each place it is mentioned in the process. When clicked, the definition appears, as shown in Figure B.9.

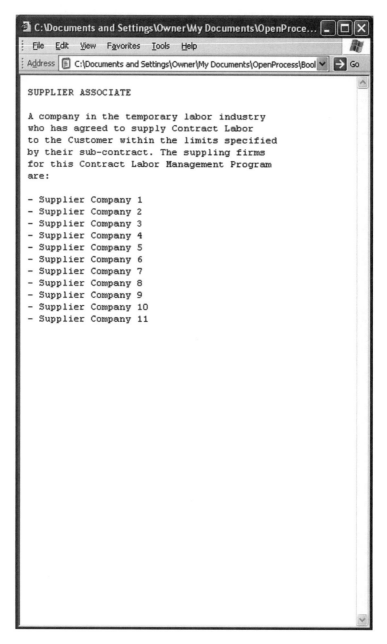

Figure B.9. A glossary term that appears in the work area.

B.10. KEYWORD HYPERLINK TO DOCUMENTATION

Sometimes, the process has already been documented in memos or policy statements from corporate executives. There may also be critical supporting documentation that must accompany the process. In these cases, a keyword hyperlink to the document will suffice, as shown in Figure B.10.

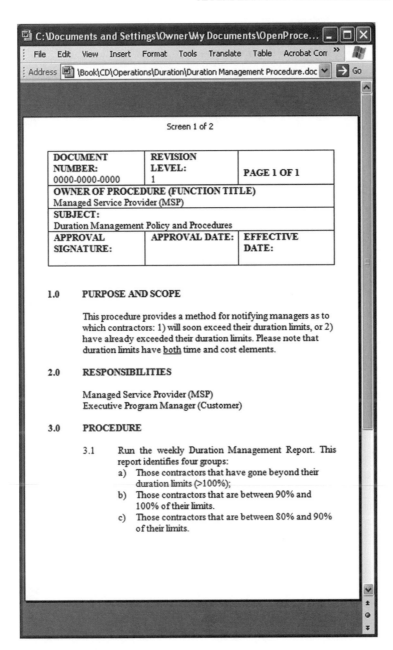

Figure B.10. A policy document that appears in the work area frame.

B.11. KEYWORD HYPERLINK TO e-FORM

When the user comes to that part of a process description where an e-form is referenced, the user simply clicks on the hyperlink to access the e-form and place it in the work area frame. The user then completes the e-form and clicks "submit" to send it on its way (Figure B.11).

C:\Documents and Settings\Owner\My Documents\OpenProce...

File   Edit   View   Insert   Format   Tools   Translate   Table   Go To   Fav »

Address 📄 uments\OpenProcess\Book\CD\Operations\Forms\Submittal Form.doc ▼ → Go

Screen 1 of 1

CANDIDATE SUBMITTAL FORM

Date Requested: _____
Requisition Number: _____
Submitter: _____

CANDIDATES TO REVIEW:

#	Name	Code	Title	Availability
1				
2				
3				
4				

MANAGER ACTION:

#	Hire	Interview	Decline	Comments
1				
2				
3				
4				

ADDITIONAL INSTRUCTIONS:
___ Hold this Search.
___ Cancel the Requisition.
___ Contact _____ for details.

[Submit]   [Cancel]

Figure B.11. An e-form for the contract labor management process.

B.12. KEYWORD HYPERLINK TO APPLICATION GUI

As discussed in Part III, if software applications are Web-based and open, then a Web-based process can invoke a software function directly without going through a menu tree. For example, imagine that you are responsible for checking all time cards at week's end.

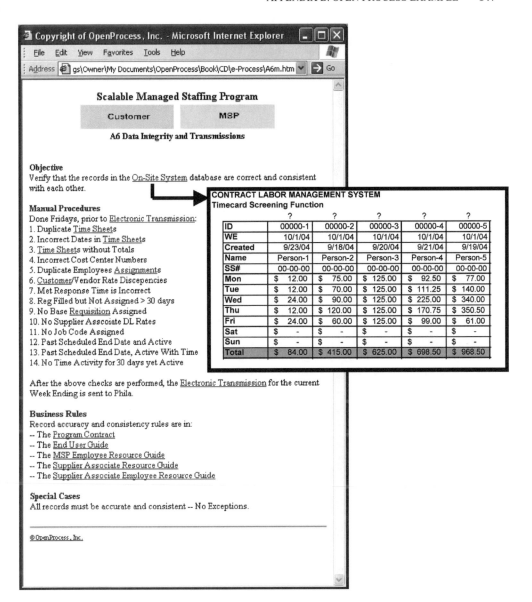

Figure B.12. How users invoke only the software functions they need.

You go to the process for doing that function, click on the system hyperlink, and are given just that GUI. This interaction can be depicted as in Figure B.12.

B.13. KEYWORD HYPERLINK TO REPORT

An effective solution will provide up-to-the-minute information and will organize the data into time frames that make sense to the business. For example, weekly labor utilization is a crucial report (Figure B.13).

	A	B	C	D	E	F	G	H
				fx	Div			
1	Div	Labor	Hours	FTE	Cost	$/HR	% Hours	
2	Div-A	Skill-A	61	4.19	$1,373.85	$22.52	1.05%	
3	Div-A	Skill-B	239	16.41	$2,230.97	$9.35	4.11%	
4	Div-A	Skill-C	113	7.78	$1,390.13	$12.29	1.95%	
5	Div-A	Skill-S	25	1.74	$195.43	$7.73	0.43%	
6	Div-A	Skill-I	65	4.50	$2,787.94	$42.59	1.13%	
7	Div-A	Skill-T	58	3.96	$881.48	$15.31	0.99%	
8	Div-B	Skill-A	7	0.46	$151.95	$22.90	0.11%	
9	Div-B	Skill-B	4	0.25	$51.88	$14.27	0.06%	
10	Div-B	Skill-E	8	0.53	$347.26	$45.47	0.13%	
11	Div-B	Skill-P	6	0.40	$295.38	$50.77	0.10%	
12	Div-C	Skill-A	284	19.52	$7,837.89	$27.60	4.89%	
13	Div-C	Skill-B	131	9.03	$1,385.34	$10.55	2.26%	
14	Div-C	Skill-E	157	10.79	$8,556.11	$54.51	2.70%	
15	Div-C	Skill-S	67	4.63	$2,885.87	$42.90	1.16%	
16	Div-C	Skill-P	63	4.33	$3,815.51	$60.52	1.08%	
17	Div-C	Skill-I	15	1.04	$335.21	$22.07	0.26%	
18	Div-D	Skill-A	77	5.32	$1,362.80	$17.63	1.33%	
19	Div-D	Skill-B	48	3.29	$521.91	$10.89	0.82%	
20	Div-D	Skill-D	14	0.95	$268.34	$19.42	0.24%	
21	Div-D	Skill-G	29	2.00	$524.92	$18.04	0.50%	
22	Div-D	Skill-E	8	0.54	$313.30	$40.07	0.13%	
23	Div-D	Skill-S	20	1.34	$178.20	$9.14	0.34%	
24	Div-D	Skill-P	25	1.73	$1,321.69	$52.68	0.43%	
25	Div-D	Skill-S	15	1.03	$526.93	$35.34	0.26%	
26	Div-E	Skill-A	353	24.23	$8,942.55	$25.37	6.06%	
27	Div-E	Skill-B	383	26.34	$3,591.64	$9.38	6.59%	
28	Div-E	Skill-D	146	10.01	$5,475.53	$37.60	2.51%	
29	Div-E	Skill-E	351	24.10	$14,806.31	$42.23	6.03%	
30	Div-E	Skill-S	59	4.04	$198.39	$3.38	1.01%	
31	Div-E	Skill-P	206	14.13	$10,876.03	$52.92	3.54%	
32	Div-E	Skill-I	30	2.04	$1,226.98	$41.27	0.51%	
33	Div-E	Skill-T	63	4.31	$914.50	$14.60	1.08%	
34	Div-F	Skill-E	16	1.08	$491.55	$31.44	0.27%	
35	Div-F	Skill-T	126	8.63	$3,159.52	$25.17	2.16%	
36		Totals:	3268	224.65	$89,223.29	$27.30	56.22%	
37								
38								
39								

Figure B.13. A sample weekly report of contract labor utilization (data randomly generated).

ABOUT THE AUTHOR

David A. Marca is Lead Faculty at the Boston Campus of the University of Phoenix. He has published six books and 20 technical papers on electronic commerce, groupware, workflow, systems analysis, and software engineering, and holds a U.S. Patent in workflow technology. Marca is also President of OpenProcess, Incorporated, an e-Business consulting firm he established in 1997. His clients have included Siemens, Oracle, Dupont, Nokia, Banco Nacionale de Mexico, Chemical Bank, Mass Financial Services, AdvancedPCS, Serono, Olivetti, General Instruments, Southern New England Telecom, Boeing, Kongsberg Vaapenfabrik, the State of North Carolina, the State of New York, and the United States Air Force, Army and Navy.

A staffing industry professional since 1996, Marca consults to Fortune 2000 firms in the areas of business strategy, solution architecture, and project management for contract labor management solutions. He provides contract negotiation, executive leadership, team building, business metrics, program management, process reengineering, solution design, training development and delivery, and project management.

Formerly, Marca was Director of Operations, worldwide, for CDI Corporation, one of the 10 largest United States staffing firms, Deputy Director of Computers for Broome County, New York, and Senior R&D Manager for Digital Equipment Corporation.

Marca holds a B.S. (Hons) in Computer Science from Potsdam University, and an M.S. in Computer Systems from Binghamton University. He is a member of the Institute of Electrical and Electronic Engineers (IEEE), the Association for Computing Machinery (ACM), and the Project Management Institute (PMI).

INDEX